ECOLOGICAL
MORALITY

Also by Bruce Allsopp

CIVILIZATION, THE NEXT STAGE
EDUCATION AND SELF EXPRESSION
THE PROFESSIONAL ARTIST IN A CHANGING SOCIETY
THE FUTURE OF THE ARTS
STYLE IN THE VISUAL ARTS
THE STUDY OF ARCHITECTURAL HISTORY
Etc.

Novels.
POSSESSED
THE NAKED FLAME
TO KILL A KING

BRUCE ALLSOPP

ECOLOGICAL MORALITY

FREDERICK MULLER LTD

*First published in Great Britain 1972
by Frederick Muller Limited, 110 Fleet Street,
London, E.C.4*

Copyright © 1972 Bruce Allsopp

SBN 584 10066 3

Printed by Northumberland Press Limited, Gateshead

Contents

Preface

This book is not written in anger: it is too late for that. There has been so much destruction, and so many clever people have assailed the old values, that mankind is sick through being purged with negative criticism. We have been taught to despise and encouraged to hate. We are perilously divided. Not only mankind is threatened by our failure: by our lack of understanding, our divisions and our greed we imperil the rest of nature upon Earth. This is sober fact.

But I have not written a prophecy of doom nor do I believe that simply by the revival of old values and adherence to old ideas of morality and religion we can solve our urgent problems of living with ourselves and the rest of nature. The conditions of our time are unique and require new ideas, new values and a new morality commensurate with the unprecedented challenges which confront mankind.

Conservation, a rearguard action to save as much as we can, is only a stop-gap. Industrial man cannot go back to a purely rural economy by any acceptable political means unless it happens as a result of a major but not total disaster. We should not court a cataclysm as an escape from ineffectual despair. We should not contemplate abandoning all the good that has come from the industrial revolution, but to save what we have worked so hard to achieve we must realize that the industrial revolution was not eternal and we are already in an age of biological revolution. Continual expansion of the economy is a mirage and we shall have to learn to live more economically. Unless we have new moral standards the social stresses caused by inevitable changes will tear civilization to pieces.

We have lost faith in long-term planning. We no longer plant acorns in confidence that the oak trees will be of value to our great-grandchildren. Our generation is alone in all history because it has lost confidence in the future. This is a moral failure and the purpose of this book is to lay a few foundations upon which a new faith may be built. There are two basic needs. The first is to understand that all men belong to a single species and divisions based upon class, colour or creed are artificial and damaging. The second is that the resources of Earth are finite and must be cultivated, not exploited.

Chapter One

The Background

The growth of democracy, coinciding with industrialization and greatly increased population, has led to a relationship between the individual and the state which is no longer acceptable. The hydrogen bomb and the population explosion present new challenges to thought and each threatens the very existence of man. The old ideas of revolution no longer relate to the realities of our predicament and despair leads to a defeatist kind of anarchism. Lacking a sense of social purpose people see cultivation of selfhood as a way of life and find that 'the system' whatever its political complexion, while it often encourages the self through education denies it opportunities of adult fulfilment.

A new 'generalized selfishness' has replaced the 'special selfishness' of a ruling class and we have become a rapacious society. We are obsessed by the idea of working for higher standards of living but these elude us and we see the quality of our lives depreciating as we plunder the resources of the earth and pollute our environment. Neither religion nor historical determinism relate adequately to our condition which is new and was unforeseen. We need a new and realistic ethical basis.

IN BERTRAND RUSSELL's words, *Man is not a solitary animal, and so long as social life survives, self-realiza-*

tion cannot be the supreme principle of ethics.[1] More than three centuries earlier John Donne had written, *No man is an island, entire of itself; every man is a piece of the Continent, a part of the main.*[2] Between Donne and Russell ideas, philosophies and social movements came into being which emphasized the importance of selfhood but concurrently new concepts in political and social philosophy substituted, for old types of government by a single or collective ruler, the notion of the state as an entity having rights over the individual which were conceived as being derived from the collective will of the people. This seemed to be an improvement, but modern self-conscious man is discovering in the idea of the state a new kind of tyranny. The ruling state is thought of as representing society, to which the individual has moral obligations, but these are presumed upon by the state in ways which become increasingly irksome. The moral bases of the citizen's duties and the state's authority become more and more obscure and our problems are be-devilled by entirely new challenges to the very exist-ence of man.

Pre-eminent among these new challenges to human thought and feeling are the thermo-nuclear bomb and the population explosion. If any human group chooses to use the ultimate weapons of modern war, no matter how 'good' their cause may be, there is little doubt that the human race and most other forms of life will be destroyed and only the super-optimist can believe that a new phase of evolution towards something better than man will then begin. Or the earth may just be-come sterile; a beautiful place with clouds, sunsets, rainbows and wonderful effects of light and shade on the mountains and seas with nobody to see them. This at least is a clean ending but the 'biological time bomb' poses the possibility that mankind will go rotten through multiplicity and that the end will come, not by wholesome fire and radiation, but by the degeneration of man into collective insanity.

In this context it may seem that the dispute between socialism and capitalism becomes trivial, like Nero fiddling while Rome burned, and the romantic dream of solution by revolution which has haunted human minds, especially those of the young, since Rousseau, is 'a tale told by an idiot, full of sound and fury signifying nothing'.[3]

The problem is complicated by the fact that on the earth today we have all kinds of societies, from the very primitive to the relatively civilized. There are emergent nations for which one can foresee, despite all the knowledge they may have of history, a repetition of agonies through which older nations, like France and England, have struggled over the last thousand years. We are in a hurry but we live in evolutionary time. And among the developing societies which are still only coping with the problems which beset Europe in the sixteenth century (but complicated by the effects of modern technology) one can see that for vast numbers of people the old idea of solution by social revolution is the only remedy on offer, and one is appalled by the apathy of those who have the power but lack the vision to see that anything needs doing.

There are two significant kinds of revolutionary discontent among the peoples of the world today. The one goes back a long way. It is the same sense of in-

justice and deprivation which instigated the French
Revolution of 1789, and the Russian Revolution of
1917. It has become focused upon communism which
is the main, indeed it may seem the only, hope of the
desperately poor people in socially backward countries.
Communism offers the means of displacing corrupt
and cynical capitalist regimes and is seen by those
activists who already have it as a gospel to be spread.
They believe in world revolution with the eventual
triumph of communism. This discontent is divided
between those who have communism and those who
do not, the haves considering it an obligation to help
their less fortunate comrades and the have-nots being
the traditional revolutionaries trying to improve the
lot of their own oppressed people. There is nothing
new in this kind of revolutionary and the root of
the trouble is economic, as Karl Marx made very
clear.

But the other kind of revolutionary discontent is
new and is strongest in those countries where there
is relatively little economic hardship, where labour is
organized and industries flourish, where there is a
great deal of wealth which allows most people to
enjoy a relatively high standard of living by world
standards. These are the so-called advanced countries
and the discontent does not arise from deprivation
but from lack of faith, from disgust with the mess we
seem to be making, from the realization that the old
faith in the inevitability of progress was illusory. For
some people in the advanced countries of the capitalist
west communism also has a strong appeal, partly out
of sympathy with the oppressed and partly because of
intellectual convincement. But the main body of dis-

content is not focused upon any creed or party. It is generalized and includes socialism in its disillusion. None of the old faiths speak to its condition; the old moral and social codes are questioned. Many brilliant minds have pulled down the old fabric of belief and new events, not least the invention of the atomic bomb, have created new and baffling challenges. Ultimately this kind of discontent seems to lead to the type of anarchism which seeks to destroy the present set-up and see what comes up out of the ruins because we have no idea what to do. An intermediate stage is the so-called permissive society. This is partly a genuine expression of toleration based upon respect for other people's personality, customs and beliefs but it is also, in part, an abdication of responsibility. Insofar as we recognize that permissiveness involves greater and not less responsibility for the individual it seems to be a step forward but when it is no more than laziness or an expression of despair (what does it matter anyway?) it reflects the lack of faith in any values whatsoever, even purely selfish values, which is the disease of our age. It also seems to imply 'some-one who permits' and points to 'Big Brother' our twentieth-century bogey man.

At the personal level, much modern thinking and even more of modern practice in the attitudes of individuals to their environment, to other people and to their job is based upon the idea of realizing oneself and it tends to follow that society is the milieu in which one may do this. Thus the obligation is placed upon 'society' to facilitate self-realization rather than upon the individual to contribute to society. It may be argued that the best society is that which gives most individuals the best chance to make the most of themselves but it would appear that, where the emphasis is placed upon self-fulfilment, society is weakened in its power to provide the milieu in which self-fulfilment is possible. This is demonstrated in practice in modern industrialized societies where concentration upon economic goals leads to a brief and beguiling improvement in standards and then to a general impoverishment of the quality of living. In such societies self-realization is considered to be related to earnings, and money is the key to opportunity. Education based upon the cult of self-development (equality of educational opportunity) ironically prepares children for a world in which self-fulfilment becomes increasingly difficult. The missing component is the feed-back from self to society.

But the society of *generalized* selfishness has replaced one in which the relationship of self and society was even more distorted. When our modern ideas of liberty and equality were being nurtured in the eighteenth century a small minority were able to cultivate their own selfhood by the exploitation of the rest of the human race; by oppressive working conditions and desperate poverty in the more advanced countries and by slavery in the backward countries which were being opened up for exploitation. The élitist aspects of the ethics of Aristotle suited the wealthy. Their culture, their language, their architecture, their art were heavily spiced with classicism. Greek and Roman writers formed the basis of an educational system which set the gentry apart and far above ordinary people—the *plebs*. This was a society of *specialized* selfishness.

It has been said that Christianity was a religion for slaves. It was changed into a religion for rulers. Then the romantic movement coincided with and to some extent effected another great change which gave emphasis to the equality of men in the sight of God and eventually to the belief that, since God cared for all men alike, it was in accordance with his will that they should all have equal opportunity for self-development.[4] Unhappily, and despite the blood-bath of the French Revolution, the romantic cult of freedom for the self suited the rising class of industrial exploiters, the owners of the 'dark satanic mills', the coal owners, the slave traders and the like, all enterprising men who laid the foundations of modern industrial society and were blessed with unshakable confidence in their mission to be rich, and in all fairness to many of them, to enrich society. There was a good deal of idealism in the nineteenth-century industrialist but he had greedy notions of what should be a fair reward for his own labours.

Socialists have rightly concentrated upon the horror of the exploitation of human beings during the industrial revolution and there has seemed to be no point in mentioning the fact that the standard of living did rise for nearly everybody and certainly the death rate, especially the infant death rate, fell dramatically. An industrial proletariat was created and made aware of itself as such. Through organization and co-operation, through awareness of itself as a class engaged in a class war, it has substantially improved the living standards of working people as distinct from and to a large extent at the expense of, the ruling class which is gradually merging into the managerial class with a notable blurring of the reasons for traditional animosities. While the old-style capitalist does still exist, and remains dominant in some countries, the socialist who fulminates against the capitalist system in countries such as Britain may well find that the principal shareholders for whose benefit he is working are union funds, insurance companies and charities of various kinds as well as a vast number of 'ordinary people' who have small investments in industry. The distinction in capitalist countries is increasingly between workers and management and in communist countries things are not so very different, certainly not so different as to be worth all the fuss and hostility between two systems which are both exploiting labour and the environment for immediate economic advantage.

We live in the age of the *rapacious society* and we are only just becoming aware of the fact that the exploitation and pollution of the earth's resources constitutes an even more serious threat to human society than the old exploitation of men by men. This was foreseen by such visionaries as Blake whose poem, *Jerusalem*[5] (set to music by Parry), has spoken to millions against western industrial societies' headlong pursuit of wealth at all costs. The language is symbolic and mystical. It is totally out of tune with the ideologies of modern materialistic people but the message gets through and speaks to the fundamental doubts we have about the validity of the rapacious society.

Many people are aware that we are going wrong, but the terrible thing about our concentration upon industrial production to raise the standard of living is, that by its partial success, its improvement of housing, nutrition, health, etc., it has sparked off the population explosion which threatens very quickly to demean all human standards of living. It has created automatic systems of production which displace workers and give rise to nightmares of electronic installations which take over from man as a producer, leaving him without meaning. These science-fiction dreams challenge our habitual outlook, our preoccupation with man-the-worker[6] and force us back to the questions of what life is about. What is the future of man? Most of us have our heads bowed, our eyes cast down and our feet habitually plodding a treadmill which no longer needs to exist. The great political division of our time, between socialism and capitalism, assumes on both sides that the treadmill is a necessity, that man is justified by work. We need to raise our eyes and see something beyond. We need new values, and having seen what these are we need to fashion a new morality based upon them as previous moralities have been based upon the values and social necessities of tribes, peoples and nations in the past.

At first sight it might be thought that the problem ahead was how to live with leisure, how to organize a society which would not be based upon productive work, and this might lead in the direction of life, liberty and the pursuit of happiness,[7] the right of every human being to develop his own potentialities, his self, to the maximum extent possible without infringing the rights of others to do the same.

But if we pursue happiness, according to our present ideas of what happiness is, we shall require more and more material products from our automatic electronic slaves; we shall use more and more precious resources and create an increasing volume of polluting waste products. Moreover the exploitation of leisure requires much more space than the routine of our work-a-day lives, from home to office or factory and back to bed. It is already obvious in most cities that adequate facilities for leisure would occupy far more space than can be made available for them. It is not enough to continue in our present ways of enjoying ourselves and it is worth while to reflect that most of these amusements are, in their present forms, of very recent origin. The association football match is an example, with its curious psychological participation of the crowd in the activities of twenty-two players and a referee—100,023 people on about ten acres (four hectares) of land!

The use of leisure is undoubtedly a serious problem but this can only be solved in the context of new ideas, a new ethic which relates to the realities of our time which were unforeseen by social philosophers of the nineteenth century.

Chapter Two

The Functional Nature of Morality in Relation to Modern Conditions

Morality was based upon social necessity and convenience but some religions gave divine sanction to what had become customary. In competition among warring groups of men the sense of acting in accordance with divine will was a winning characteristic and communism has embraced this asset in historical determinism. But new weapons have made war too dangerous to all humanity and the population explosion likewise threatens our existence. Neither threat discriminates, as the old myth of the Judgement Day did, between good and bad. The dangers of our time are indiscriminate. It is difficult to adjust to the outlawing of war and still more difficult to accept control of breeding. This can only be done consciously and deliberately upon some ethical basis, which means that we have to make new evaluations and create a new morality.

If moralities are responses to the realities of human environments we need to look at the new and unique relationship of modern industrial man to the rest of nature. Industrialism is moving from pure profit motivation to cost-effectiveness and professional management, but its basis is economic not ecological.

THE WORD *morality* comes to us from ancient Rome, from *mores*. This is the plural of *mos* of which the

primary meaning seems to have been 'the will of a
person; self will, a person's humour, caprice, etc.'[8] and
it probably comes from the verb meare which means
to measure in the sense of measure one's way, and of
human beings to go, to pass, to go one's way. In the
plural mores becomes the way of going together, what
is customary and the idea of it meaning what is right
derives from the idea that what is customary is right.
This point is not made out of pedantry nor because
there is any great value in the derivation of a word if
in fact its usage has changed but because it may serve
to emphasize the great difference between the idea of
morality in a society, such as ancient Rome, where
the official gods were not identified with virtue and
there was general religious toleration (except in later
stages for Christians who were intolerant of other
religions) and a Christian society. We have inherited
from the nineteenth century, when people could say,
positively 'this is a Christian country', the idea that
the mores of a national group are based upon religion,
upon the will of God. The implication is that what
is moral is right and good, not merely what is customary and convenient. Christianity and Islam are the
two great religions which have most confused morality
with goodness. Under Islam the result has been a rigid
code of behaviour based upon the exigencies of a
relatively primitive desert people. Under Christianity,
which is much more flexible and permeated with
Greek philosophical thought, there has been an
attempt to reconcile the good with the godly. God is
conceived as totally good and morality becomes
behaviour which is in accordance with the will of
God. Thus mores receive divine sanction. Fortunately

the complex flexibility and inner contradictions of the Christian religion allowed a fair measure of adaptation to changing conditions. This might be criticized as hypocrisy by dogmatists or explained as the continuing revelation of God's will by those who saw that customs which had been evolved by primitive Jewish people in Old Testament times would have to change, at least in detail if not in principle. Thus, for example, polygamy was replaced by very strict monogamy, and concubinage, from being normal for men who could afford it, became sinful.

However, western nations entered the twentieth century with *mores* sponsored by Christianity. It is now notorious that the moral rigidity, often amounting to sheer cruelty, of Victorian England and large sections of North American society, was firmly based upon what were believed to be Christian principles. It is still by no means uncommon to hear of eminent judges referring to the law of God as well as of man and that vague entity which we call 'The Establishment' is something of a conspiracy to preserve the belief that its values and way of life are in accordance with the will of God and are therefore *right*.

From the Establishment point of view there is a great deal to be said for linking religion, morality and law. Looked at politically a society which can do this has a unity and strength which give considerable advantages over 'lesser breeds without the Law'.[9]

> *Here's a health to the king, a lasting peace*
> *To faction an end, to wealth increase.*[10]

If one sees the human race in terms of groups competing for survival there is no doubt that a system which
eliminates or reduces internal dissent to a minimum
is a winning characteristic. This is recognized by all
totalitarian régimes. But group unity in the face of
other groups, with competition leading to effective
war, the dominance of the stronger group and the
reduction of inferior groups, is no longer an acceptable moral basis nor is it a practicable policy. War
with hydrogen bombs, germs and unrevealed horrors
which clever but amoral scientists are cooking has to
be ruled out because it would be race suicide. The
achievement of sure peace may present innumerable
difficulties but at least the logic and the objective are
clear: we must have peace.

Pop

Reversal of the population trend is a much more
complicated problem. It could and indeed may be
brought about in the old way by a great deal of dying
and a consequent load of sorrow if we abdicate from
our responsibility and court disaster. Any less horrible
way of controlling population must depend upon man
subjecting the biological urge and instinct to *some
other order of values*. This may sound easy but in fact
it is still an unanswered question whether man is at
present capable of doing this. Put in another way,
biological man if he continues to increase in numbers
will, in the not distant future, so pollute the earth
that, despite all his technical resources, he will be
subject to catastrophe; and partly because of the lethal
effectiveness of his own technology that catastrophe
might be complete. This is a challenge to the mind of
man which is new in his history. The notion of the
day of judgement, so vividly portrayed in medieval

'doom' windows, was nothing like this because it presumed that there would be a *judgement*.

*'Tis the Last Judgement's fire must cure this place,
Calcine its clods and set my prisoners free.'*[11]

For 'the just' the day of judgement could be contemplated with awe but not despair. It was 'the sinner'
who was doomed. The nearest men have come to the
present challenge was probably in the great plagues
when they must have wondered whether any would
escape, when, as all those one loved and knew were
stricken down, the will to live was crushed under the
burden of misery. But men did survive and re-
peopled the land. Out of despair came hope and even
a renewed sense of fulfilment. Now it is different.[12]
We have come to terms with the fact that we ourselves
must make the judgement and if we fail to regulate
our own nature the consequential disaster will not
discriminate between saint and sinner or between
revolutionary and reactionary. It is difficult enough to
accept that we can no longer settle our quarrels by
force but it is even harder to understand that we must
control our breeding. Coming to terms with the bomb
is at least in line with the instinct to survive. Here we
have nature on our side though we must make a vast
change in our habits of thought and action. But to
control the 'right' to breed seems to be against nature,
indeed it *is* against the biological nature of man and
all living creatures. The ethical problems are therefore staggering but let us recognize that they are
ethical problems. We can only control population by
intention and such intention must have a foundation.

This could simply be fear, a recognition of the
ecological consequences, and if war were not ruled
out by a countervailing fear of total destruction the
old law of the survival of the fittest could apply as it
did, for example, in the closing phase of the Roman
Empire with the consequent near-destruction of
western civilization. But we dare not hope for a solution by war and we cannot welcome cholera as a
liberator and stand idly by while people die of it
because this is to deny something in ourselves with
which, in the state of being to which we have come
through ages of thought and experience, we cannot
dispense and still retain our self-respect. We cannot
be arbitrary in denying the 'right to breed' or otherwise controlling population by, for example, infanticide and compulsory euthanasia of the elderly. This
would be politically and socially impossible. We could
not create and accept an arbitrary authority with
powers of life and death. We would require an ethical
basis. In some way, as human beings, we would have
to develop a new justice and while it is conceivable
that adult lives might be judged by some criteria of
social usefulness (undesirable though this may be if
only because usefulness is undefinable), the practice of
infanticide would be intolerable within our present
concepts of justice and there seems to be practically
no hope at present of population control, on the scale
necessary, by voluntary methods. The mind boggles at
the idea of an 'illegal birth' followed by the destruction of the baby, enforced by law, but unless we can
develop a new ethic this is the direction in which we
are unhappily and inevitably tending.

The biological time bomb, unless we can de-fuse it,

threatens all standards of the value of human life at philosophical and religious levels, while it also threatens to bring about the debasement and possible extinction of life at the physical level.

This is the challenge, the new obstacle over which the human race has to pass if it is to go on. To cope with this challenge we need new tools, new *mores* based upon new reality. Western philosophy as it has come to be, does not provide these tools though it has forged some of the means by which the new tools may be made. It is idle to pretend that either philosophy or religion in their present forms can cope with the new challenge and this is generally understood by thoughtful people—hence the widespread disillusion and lack of hope. Political and economic systems as we know them do not provide answers and the projection of modern materialism into our problematical future would seem to be a sure road to disaster. Biological man must either perish or find in the human mind a new answer to this unprecedented challenge, a new evaluation, in effect a new morality.

At this stage in the argument it may be agreed that the *mores* of all human societies have been derived from what are, or were, the social necessities of each society in the environment where it sought to survive.[13] Seldom were these *mores* actually thought out; much more often they seem to have evolved out of man's response to the environmental conditions, and if they took a wrong direction probably that society failed to survive. This is fairly clear to the anthropologist who studies the beliefs and customs of primitive tribes but there is also a good deal of evidence that advanced societies, even societies on such a

scale that we can call them 'civilizations' can perish
through failure to adapt their customs, habits and
institutions to changes in the environment.[14] One of
the most recent and revealing enactments of the old
drama of forging a society took place in North
America. The wild west with its own peculiar morality
of the pioneers; its naïve faith in the inevitability of
the good man, with quick hands to his gun, winning
through; the prodigal waste of natural resources,
particularly wild life; the value-judgements of a cow-
punching community and the stiffening of religion
brought over from the old world; the deep prejudices
against Indians, Negroes and miscegenation; all these
were moral sinews of an emergent and eventually
triumphant society which was subsequently to translate
its mythology into film and then face the appalling
problems of running a modern, multi-racial, industrial society with the moral resources of pioneering
days.

But what is environment? Obviously it includes
the physical nature of the part of the earth where we
live, its rocks and streams, its climate and hence its
vegetation and natural fauna. Left alone nature
arrives at a balance which is not absolutely stable but
will vary, pulsate so to speak, as the various plant and
animal communities interact. The study of this inter-
relationship of living things in their physical environment is called *ecology*. Man may be thought of as
part of nature, and taken within this subject, but he
has become so powerful and so destructive of other
forms of life, as well as being able to manipulate
breeding so as to produce new plants and animals,
that he can and does profoundly alter the balanced

pattern. We are concerned here with man as a being who is capable of making major alterations in his environment. Some of these are done consciously, as by building houses, irrigating deserts, clearing forests or building factory estates. Equally significant is the damage man does and the mess he makes. Industrial man in particular has a foul record.

The very slightest acquaintance with ecology reveals the interaction of any community with its environment. The proliferation of an animal species, for example, may be controlled by the plant upon which it feeds and over-exploitation leads to starvation with obvious consequences for the species. Sometimes the balance is restored and the cycle begins again, but a species may be so weakened that it falls victim to predators it might otherwise resist and a critical point may be reached at which the unlikelihood of meeting and mating is such that the species becomes extinct. There is no need to labour the point that what an animal does to its environment can and usually does bounce back to affect the said animal. In doing anything to the environment we are affecting the environment in relation to ourselves. It is clear that 'the environment' is not a fixed thing; nature around us is continually being altered by what we do. Look for example at a picture of a country scene in the eighteenth century and then at the same place now. Even if it has stayed rural it has altered almost beyond recognition as a result mainly of human activity but also from natural growth of vegetation, particularly trees. If we choose a scene to which London or some other large city has spread the change, of course, is complete. Again, if we go to a coal-mining valley or

the vicinity of a chemical plant we may find sheer
desolation with a new ecological pattern of rank
weeds.

It is not sufficiently realized that historians attend
to matters which interest them and the people for
whom they write. Our view of history is coloured by
the values of the society in which we live. Some things
get left out. We may easily find out about the exploitation of labour in the nineteenth century, the growth of
legislation for public health and education and there
may be references to the resistance of the landed
aristocracy to the encroachment of industrialization
but of the long history of rural conservation there is
little mention and still less understanding of the real
sense of outrage felt by land-owners as they beheld the
rape of a rural economy which was the result of many
centuries of careful cultivation. We have only to turn
the pages of Virgil's *Georgics* (*c.*29 B.C.) which were in
part written in support of government policy to
remedy the current decay of rural conservation, to
realize that the concept of 'good husbandry' goes back
a long way. It persisted throughout the Roman Empire
and the villa estates of western Europe were carefully
integrated economic and ecological units. In Britain
the Anglo-Saxon conquest disrupted the pattern but
it was restored in the manorial system. In France, Italy
and Western Germany it continued and so did
systematic forestry. In Spain it was taken over and
developed by the Moors but fell into decay when they
were driven out by Christians. It is particularly
instructive to walk in some of the state forests of
France which were already state forests (Compiègne,
for example) under Merovingian kings in the sixth

century. They are not 'natural' forests; their beauty and their economic value are the result of at least *fifteen centuries of conservation.*

Eighteenth-century England in which the industrial revolution first took hold, had gone through an agrarian revolution whereby a great deal of common land had been brought into cultivation with considerable economic gains at the cost of much human grievance but it was an extension of *cultivation* not the rape of the countryside and the idea of continuity, of planning and planting for the future, of provident long-term management, was deeply rooted in the minds of all good landowners. Even the human family was subject to the needs of the estate which passed entirely, to the eldest son so that its integrity might be maintained (in contrast to the fairer system prevalent in Ireland where land was divided with consequent impoverishment).

Conservation of the environment and working *with* nature are essential to the agrarian economy. Planning must be seasonal for the regular crops off arable land, generational for live-stock and very long-term for timber. In the garden there are annuals and perennials, soil must be carefully worked into condition, tilth developed and sheltering hedges cultivated. Nothing is instant and profit is slow to accrue. In contrast, though there is a similar build-up of potential in industry the 'plant' is expected to go into production quickly and return on capital is implicit in the original financial arrangements. The fundamental difference is that agriculture depends upon cultivation of the land, the surface of the earth we live on, whereas industry is financed. It depends upon money which

represents goods and services. Land, it is true, can be
bought, but a tiny fraction of the money in circula-
tion represents land and the wealth of the world which
money represents is mostly man-made or ravished from
the earth. Where land values are high we find congested building, as in the City of London or Man-
hattan, the value being not in the land for what it is
but for what can be put on it in terms of rent-produc-
ing accommodation.

It is important to make the distinction between a
rural, cultivated system and an industrial cost-effective
system but we cannot put the clock back, and we certainly cannot support present populations by reverting to a rural economy. Furthermore industrialization
has brought many benefits and the ordinary worker of
today lives in far greater comfort and convenience
than kings did in earlier times. Though his living
quarters are less sumptuous than Versailles he has
many amenities in his own home which were beyond
the dreams of even Louis XIV. These, from curtain
fabrics, wallpapers and clothes to washing machines,
main drainage, radio and television are all products
of industrialization and backward countries naturally
pin their hopes of improvement upon the development of industry. In a more sinister way the attitudes
of cost-conscious industrial organization have begun
to permeate agriculture to the detriment of long-term
cultivation. Hedges and shelter belts come down to
make way for mechanization and precious soil blows
away in the wind.

Industrial society has had its stormy honeymoon. It
has brought forth abundantly and the real problems
are just beginning. There is a houseful of yowling

kids to be brought up. One may clutch at the idea of colonizing the planets but evidence accumulates that even if any of them are at all habitable by man the environmental conditions would be worse than upon Earth, which is our natural habitat and its worst deserts and jungles compare favourably with anything we are likely to find elsewhere. Anyway, why abandon this pleasant Earth because we can't organize ourselves properly? And if we did escape from our planet and our inadequacy in the face of our own weakness, would we do any better on Mars?

We cannot escape. We cannot go back. We have achieved miracles and the new challenge is to bridle the wild horse of industrialization and establish a new balance with nature so that our efforts tend towards enrichment and not, as at present, towards disaster and the loss of all we have struggled to achieve.

We cannot do this so long as we cling to the assumptions and the morality of industrialism. But when one says 'the morality of industrialism' what is it? There is no morality worth the name. Produce and grow rich. Raise the material standard of living. Maximize gain by the study of cost-effectiveness.

In crude capitalism profit was the prime motive and there are many people in business and industry who still believe that the primary object of any business is to maximize profit for its owners, its shareholders. But this is an archaism. Most large-scale industry is run by business bureaucracies and each industrial group becomes something like an ancient dukedom or kingdom, often extending across national boundaries and having its own internal social system. It distributes dividends at its discretion and with an

eye on its credit in case it wants more capital. The
phrase 'the interests of shareholders' is mouthed like
a litany but the group is a closed system, as autono-
mous as possible and socially irresponsible sometimes
to the point of complete cynicism. Much the same can
be said of state industries, both under state capitalism
and under socialism. State control over industrial
management may even be more difficult to achieve
under socialism than in nominally free economies because bureaucratic industrial management tends to
merge into government bureaucracy, the industry becoming in effect a department of state, like the army.
In non-communist states there is the tenuous safe-
guard of responsibility to a minister but the expertise
and knowledge is all in the management and government is less and less equipped to intervene.

But there must be standards by which efficiency
can be judged, malpractices put right and ineffectual
managements displaced. The new standard, which is
replacing the profit motive is *cost-effectiveness*. It is
equally applicable in a communist or a capitalist
economy and its logic is beautifully simple. It derives
straight from the profit motive but reinterprets it in
more socially acceptable terms. The creed is that it is
right to get the maximum yield from the least deploy-
ment of effort. Since everything has to be measurable
by accountants yield and effort are expressed in terms
of money. What is not quantifiable cannot be taken
into account. Values, other than money values, cannot be expressed in money so we have the lunatic
result that value judgements cannot be evaluated and
therefore cannot be taken into account. This is so
absurd that some practical examples must be given as

evidence that such idiocy is practised, by sane people.

In a planning appeal efforts were made to save a building of architectural distinction. The value put by the planners upon the building was the cost of moving it to another site which, according to their figures, was too much. In appeal it was argued that the building was of historic and artistic importance, an irreplaceable part of the city's heritage and the work of its most distinguished architect. All these were value judgements, mere opinion it was argued by the authority's counsel.

An architect included a piece of sculpture in his design for a school. Provision had been made by the education authority for the inclusion of money to be spent on sculpture but, owing to inflation, the lowest tender for building the school exceeded the estimate so the architect was instructed to omit the sculpture because it was unnecessary. In other words, its value, other than its actual cost, could not be brought into account.

Much of the dreary character of modern architecture derives from concentration upon cost-effectiveness. It is virtually designed by accountants. This applies even more to government-financed building than it does in the 'private sector' and it has long been the practice to build publicly financed housing at the lowest possible cost of providing the minimally acceptable standards of accommodation. It is a sad truth about socialist authorities that they have consistently practised according to the principle that the cheapest is good enough for the poor, quality and beauty being only for those who can afford them. This is exactly what the despised nineteenth-century industrialists did when they built what became slums. And of course most slum-clearance schemes are incipient slums.

A final example may be given from *The Times* report of the British Association meeting in Swansea, Park.[15]

A view from officialdom responsible for controlling exploitation was given yesterday by Mr. T. M. Thomas, principal scientific officer, Welsh Office. He said the fact that proposed workings might be situated in a national park, or in an area of outstanding natural beauty or a green belt, was not in itself sufficient to justify refusal of permission.

The intrinsic beauty, peace and quiet of a district constituted important factors to be taken into account, but mineral workings on land of high agricultural quality were likely to meet with the strongest objections.

Mr. Thomas's comments had to be seen in the light of the controversies about mineral exploitation in Wales, particularly those centred on Rio Tinto-Zinc prospecting in the Snowdonia National Park.[15]

In the location of airports, in the siting of factories, the discharge of effluents, in the regulation of noise, in the institution of safety standards, it has generally been assumed, in the rapacious society, that efficiency (meaning cost-effectiveness) must have priority and anyone who denies this is 'against progress'. But more and more people are becoming aware that other values, such as beauty, safety, peace and quiet, historical associations, the rights of individuals, all of them values which cannot be quantified, must be taken effectively into account. It is now obvious that much 'development' is destructive and that by getting cost out of all proportion we are devaluing our lives. The realists are those who see man in his ecological context. The reactionaries are those who cling to the dogmas of the rapacious industrial society.

Chapter Three

Conditions for an Ecological Morality

Man is not only a social animal but as a species he has to fit into an ecological context. The nineteenth-century idea of man as distinct from the rest of nature must be replaced. Present political confrontations distract from the major problems of mankind. Ecological awareness and the roots of an ecological morality are actually developing but the threat of war and preparation for it make the necessary action and attitudes impossible. A weakness of Marxism is its belief in war and capitalism is committed to exploitation. Man is a single species and there is growing awareness of this essential fact.

Peace is essential and the abandonment of war will create an economic dislocation which will be a catalyst. Belief in peace, based upon recognition and fear of the nature of war in modern conditions will create a new climate of opinion and political possibility. Nationalism is already breaking down.

Believing in progress Marx was able to dispense with ethical considerations and foresee an economic revolution but his deterministic view of history ignored the possibility of new factors. Materialism, in a new context of more productive industry and increasing population, has created new problems and the old relationship between work and wealth has to be reconsidered in terms of values which cannot be owned or transferred, which are communally shared and are being destroyed.

THE NECESSITY can be stated as, *to create a balanced relationship between man and his environment*. Two problems immediately arise: what is a balanced relationship and what is the environment? Taking the second first, the environment is both external and internal. Our internal environment, our own natures and the 'collective unconscious' must be considered later. The question of balance between man and all the other living species must come first. How does one evaluate a human being against a butterfly, a squirrel or a swallow? If the man is Napoleon or Shakespeare, Einstein or Castro, is it a different problem from comparing with a thalidomide baby (a by-product of cost-effective thinking) or a criminal lunatic?

If I were God I might well prefer swallows, squirrels and butterflies to man, but man, as a species conceives God in his own image (*Genesis* 1.27). The only ethic which could possibly gain acceptance among men would be one which ministered to man's belief in the supremacy of man. But man is physically dependent upon other forms of life, upon corn and upon animal flesh. At the lowest possible level he is dependent upon sharing the earth with the forms of life upon which he feeds. Not all land is capable of growing corn and if it does not grow corn it may grow other plants. Most of the earth, if it will grow corn will do so only with careful cultivation. Modern grain crops are the product of careful breeding and selection of forms which are suited to particular localities. We are committed to a variety of vegetation. The animals upon which we feed are dependent upon vegetation for their food. They commit us to a greater variety of vegetation. All this is at the lowest possible survival level. We use trees for timber to make furniture, paper, etc., grasses and wood pulp to make paper upon which to convey our ideas by print; trees again to make cellulose, and coal and oil which derive from an unrepeatable vegetation of long ago to give us power, dyes, gas, wax, innumerable derivatives from the stored-up capital of millions of years of sunlight irradiating the vegetation on the earth's surface. In a lump of coal, a litre of petroleum, a handful of lime, a block of peat or a string of coral beads we have the physical legacy of thousands of lives. To recreate the stone that is taken from Derbyshire hills and turned into cement in a single day would take millions of years. These are the dry facts of the geography lesson at school but they are also eternal truths about ourselves, about the world we live in, truths to kindle the imagination and command our respect. It has taken millions of years to create our environment and we are expending it prodigally knowing, if we stop to think, that what we use could not be replaced within any time-span which is meaningful in relation to the whole of human history.

Ancient man, in his ignorance, reverenced the earth; we, with our scientific knowledge have all the more reason to do so. Sophisticated people despise anthropomorphism (the attribution of human form to spiritual powers) but it was much better to conceive the earth as a mother goddess than to treat our environment the way we do. And if the neutral word *environment* is

incapable of evoking the necessary response in us, and
if we have no better way of thinking, then we would
do well to go back to the concept of Mother Earth.
We seem to need to conceptualize in order to think
and feel about such relationships as that between ourselves and nature. The word *nature* itself is such a
conceptualization, so is *environment*, but in our eager-
ness as modern men in a scientific age to get rid of
superstition we have lost certain necessary modes of
expression. If *nature* is '*the material world as a whole*'
it does not have the same meaning as *Nature* being
'*the power underlying all phenomena in the material
world*'. Both definitions are to be found in a dictionary. The former is more in tune with scientific thought
but the latter recognizes the *force* which is implicit
in any relationship. It also acknowledges the *fact* that,
whatever linguistic quibbles we may indulge in, nature
does hit back. Our environment is not soft clay which
will take any shape the sculptor's hands have the skill
to give it. It is resilient and powerful. The power is
real, in the ordinary practical sense of the word real.
It is effective and, like a human personality, to a large
extent predictable. But it does not behave like an
ordinary physical force, such as gravity. It consists of
a multiplicity of relationships—plants, insects, soil,
weather, animals, instincts, competition for survival,
chemical reactions, viruses, radiation and so on.
Whereas the engineer can work out mechanical or
electronic problems with considerable accuracy because he can define his problem and restrict it to a
few variables, the relationship of man with nature
cannot be so defined. What, for example, are the long
term consequences of turning the American Great

Lakes into cess-pools such as have never existed before?
With the old forms of life destroyed and the water
polluted by an unpredictable mixture of organic and
inorganic waste, still surrounded by living communities, including human beings in congested towns, it
would be a rash man indeed who would predict with
confidence what mutations may occur, both at the
physical level and in the minds of men who remember
fishing and swimming in these waters.

But we should be on our guard against dividing
the world into nature on the one hand and man on
the other. The dead Lake Ontario is just as much a
part of nature as the live Lake Ullswater,[16] but man
as a part of nature has turned one into a cess-pool and
the other, by careful conservation, into a source of
drinking water and a recreational centre. But the distinction between man and *the rest of* nature is valid
to this extent, that man has a power to affect everything else which, so far as we know, no other conscious species, capable of deliberate action, has or has
ever had. Thus the distinction, beloved of the nineteenth century and deeply rooted in the ethic of the
industrial revolution, between man and nature, is
something to be reckoned with and got rid of. In
1849 Matthew Arnold could feel virtuous and progressive in writing

Man must begin, know this, where Nature ends
Nature and man can never be fast friends.[17]

It has taken a hundred years to bring home the lesson
that man is, and must be, and cannot be anything
other than part of nature, and his relationship with

the rest of nature, with what we now call his environment, is now his greatest problem.

But before man can effectively tackle this problem he must abandon his present political preoccupations and divisions which make effective action impossible. The confrontation of America and Russia, of Communism and a 'Free Economy' is a distraction, an evasion of the main issue which now confronts the human race and ought to reduce our political and economic squabbles to a domestic level. But politicians on both sides have a vested interest in prolonging the present disputes if only because they have no alternative band-waggon upon which to climb. The real question is how man can continue to live a satisfactory life on Earth and both America and Russia have geared their economies to the belief that only one of them has the answer when in fact neither has begun to tackle the essential problem.

In so far as economics can contribute to the solution of the world ecological problem (and clearly it must be an important factor) the pursuit of wealth and a higher standard of living, no matter how it is distributed socially, will aggravate, not solve the problem. We must consider 'the economy' in a new context and with its old meaning of good housekeeping; and, while admitting the validity of much in the socialist faith, we must face the fact that socialism as such has not caught up with the modern problem. Capitalism, as now understood, seems to be ideologically opposed to conservation and committed to exploitation.

Thus it would seem that there is no existing political system or outlook which, as it stands, could take over the problems of ecology. To create a new political

climate we would need a new underlying motivation,
a new concept of man in nature, and a new morality.

An ecological ethic must apply to individual
behaviour and to organization of social groups, such
as nations or industries, but many of the major
problems necessitate international agreement and are
world-wide. An obvious example is atmospheric pollution. Another is the conservation of the seas and a
third is population movement and control. The first
two are of the kind which can conceivably be solved
by international agreement and there is already a
wide-spread belief that it is wrong for one country's
government to explode bombs which will pollute the
atmosphere of other countries. There is even a growing belief that it is *wrong* for one country to shoot or
trap birds migrating over their territory between two
other countries (France has come in for much blame
in this respect) and though the means of enforcement
are lacking the growth of a new *moral* opinion is en-
couraging. But the problems which concern population are likely to be extremely difficult.

Even at the level of local urban politics it took a
very long time for the people in the richer parts of a
town to accept the fact that slums were a danger to
their own health and safety, to realize in fact that the
welfare of a community is indivisible, and even now
there are many who do not accept this. For example
the commuter who uses his own car pleads for better
roads and parking facilities but he is indifferent to
the health hazards of insanitary and overcrowded
public transport, to long queues without shelter from
rain and wind, the unnecessary fatigue and spread of
infections. After his journey in a personal conveyance

to his office the fortunate car owner catches 'flu from someone who caught it on yesterday's bus to work and gave it every chance to develop while standing in the rain for half an hour because the first two buses home were full. The example is perhaps trite but it serves to emphasize that in ordinary everyday life, anywhere, everyone affects everyone else.

At the international level, war has always been a factor of great ecological significance. In the nineteenth century, particularly after the publication of Darwin's *The Origin of Species by Natural Selection* (1859), it was commonly argued that war was a natural and beneficial means of ensuring that the better races of man should overcome inferior races. In fact war was seen as a beneficial instrument of what we now call ecology. The irrefutable answer to this view was put in an essay by Santayana which deserves to be better known than it is.[18] The first world war of 1914-18 destroyed millions of young men, the cream of a generation, seriously weakening the white race against its supposed competitors, not by war with them but by war between white and white. From a global point of view, which is rare if not impossible for a person actually to have, this might be a 'good thing' but certainly no western man was disposed to see it that way. The second world war of 1939-45 was less destructive of life in actual battles but it unleashed a lot of horrors which profoundly shocked western man's faith in man. The invention of the atomic bomb and of germ warfare has now revealed—except to those who will not see—that whatever war may have been in the past, it would now be an ecological disaster, perhaps, indeed probably, the ultimate disaster. It must be ruled out

of our thinking as a possible way of achieving anything. In our present condition, whatever our political
views, no matter how deep our sense of injustice and
our desire to *fight* against what we think is wrong,
violence must be abandoned. It is no longer a valid
way of combat.

No doubt there are many sincere reasons for believing that war is sometimes necessary but in the modern
world there are two overriding reasons why it must
be ruled out. Any war may escalate into total war,
and once war has started conditions inherent in the
nature of war may arise whereby one side may have
to choose between extinction and using the ultimate
weapons. No war between major powers could in
practice stop short of using weapons which would
destroy mankind. The other reason is that so long as
war is contemplated and therefore prepared for, the
vital ecological problems cannot be effectively tackled.
The reasons for being against war are no longer idealistic: they are plain, down to earth practical reasons
concerned with the basic will to survive. This is the
stuff upon which a practical morality can be founded
but if war has to be abandoned, and a great change
in human relationships is to be brought about—as
must happen—then there is only one other force which
has proved effective in human history as a means of
bringing men together and generating the necessary
energy. This force has usually been manifested in what
we call a religion, but its most recent exemplification
is Marxism which has the characteristic of religions,
that it has absorbed into itself a great deal of which
its founder (who is on record as having said he was
not a Marxist) would not have approved and much

that is not directly traceable to his teaching. In the modern context the weakness of all forms of Marxism is their belief in war. Making it a war between classes and between socialist countries and capitalist countries does not mitigate this fatal flaw. But the success of Marxism is *despite* its acceptance of war and *because* of its hold over men's minds. Much of its teaching inspires belief, belief in its goodness and validity. Because of belief it has had remarkable victories over human selfishness, cupidity and inertia. It is possible that Marxism could change to become a great ecological movement but it may have gone too far, and become too much a doctrine, to be able to effect the necessary changes of outlook, and the new need is so great and so overwhelmingly important, and demands such fundamental changes in human attitudes that the ecological movement will probably have to be something on its own, superseding both Marxism and capitalism. It is to be hoped that adherents of both will go along with it but the vested interests in both are formidable.

There is one more argument about war which it will be appropriate to consider at this stage. It takes account of the fact that in the ecological set-up many species compete for survival so why should man be the exception? Man is not the exception. Man as a species is at risk, NOT from attack by other species but from destroying the rest of nature upon which he depends. The challenge is to humanity as such to survive and war, for the reasons given above, threatens his survival. Man is no longer fighting other species for survival: he is immensely powerful over them and has to learn, against all the oldest predatory

instincts, to conserve, to keep the balance, leave
enough over for other species and not hog the world
for himself because if he does he will be destitute.
Rather interestingly hunting people have long ago
realized that conservation was necessary, hence the
game laws. Paradoxically some of the best conservation is done by hunters for the reason that they want
to be able to continue hunting, so they are provident.
Humanity as a whole needs a better motive, a stronger
one to overcome all the inevitable opposition, and the
strongest motive exists if we believe that conservation
and an ecological morality are necessary for the survival of the human race.

The primary condition for an ecological ethic or
morality is that man should abandon the old idea that
the human race is an independent ecological system
of competing ethnic and social groups and that we
should accept as a fact that man is a single species
which has to fit into the total ecological system. This
is implicit in the behaviour of most species of animals
and birds. Man ought to be able to manage it. Slight
differences of skin and hair colour, small variations of
physiognomy, variations in religion, social customs,
art forms, language and economic standards are not
important and most of the lore and animosity associated with them are prejudiced rubbish. They have
acquired a specious significance because they have
been made into excuses and symbols in man's competitive struggle. The modern upsurge among young
people of disgust against race-prejudice is a step towards recognition of man as a single ecological species.
It may well be a natural instinctive feeling towards

survival. There is no reason why even modern man should not have such instincts and they should be recognized.

Chapter Four

The Garden Analogue

Political parties are means of achieving purposes which were not originated by politicians. It is no use looking to existing political organizations, in their present form, for the implementation of ecological policies. The immense problems of re-integrating man in a balance with nature may be approached by using a garden as a model because a garden is a small ecologically balanced system which man directs. We notice the significance of gardens in mythology and literature. Anarchy and cultivation are incompatible. Man as a gardener directs and participates but he is an element in the ecosystem and works *with* nature. The garden has its own rules which are not morals in our ordinary sense; they are of the *if you do this that will happen* kind. Value judgements have to be made. These are of two kinds, namely, those within the ecology of the garden and those in relation to the world outside which can intrude and destroy the garden. The garden is not a pattern for human affairs but does indicate the kind of thinking we need.

HAVING considered war and economics it might seem appropriate that we should next turn to politics but all that need be said for the moment on this subject is that no existing political system or organization has anything to offer. Politics is a *means*, not an objective. The kind of politics we need is one that will achieve a balanced and beneficial relationship between man and the rest of nature, but these are empty words until we have considered and discovered the nature of such a balanced relationship and shown that it is better than our present rapacious state of existence.

There is little to be learned from the kind of naturalism propounded by Rousseau and his followers whose concept of nature was sentimental and misleading. Modern science has given us a completely new vision of the nature of things both animate and inanimate. We may acknowledge that eighteenth-century thinkers had a prophetic glimpse of the value of harmony with nature, but there is so much new knowledge that we must start afresh and it is plain that social-political thought in the twentieth century has been mainly confined to alternative methods of continuing the progress of rapacious man. Where conservation has been the policy of a régime it has been conceived as the preservation of existing orders and values rather than the creation of a new attitude to the environment. So we start with no scheme of thinking, such as exists for socialists, and we can look neither to political establishments nor to any religion, nor to an accepted philosophy of living for basic values and related systems of thought.

The kind of balance we are thinking about did, it is true, exist as a natural phenomenon until man upset it by industrialization and applied scientific knowledge. But this was something 'given' so to speak, not contrived, and simply by being more numerous and having so much power and knowledge we are debarred from going back. We have lost that for ever and it must be admitted that we have got rid of a lot that was bad, cruel and dreary as well as making trouble for ourselves. Unless 'Nature' intervenes with some catastrophe such as a deadly mutation of the virus of the common cold, or we create a disaster by our own folly and incompetence, the new order, the new balance of nature, must be something created by man. To conceive this balance is extremely difficult and rather than wrestle directly with the problem it will be best to begin with an analogue. This will involve a digression to consider what might be a model for our thinking.

Prosaically described, a garden is '*a plot of land devoted to the cultivation of flowers, fruit and vegetables for use and ornament in the domestic economy, or forming arrangements for external scenery and for personal recreation*'.[19] A garden is, in fact a small ecologically balanced system in which man participates, to his practical and aesthetic advantage. It is the *kind* of thing we are looking for.

The garden is an archetypal symbol. In Jewish mythology it was the Garden of Eden.

But there went up a mist from the earth, and watered the whole face of the ground.

And the LORD God formed man of the dust of the ground, and breathed into his nostrils the breath of life; and man became a living soul.

And the LORD God planted a garden eastward in Eden: and there he put the man whom he had formed.

And out of the ground made the LORD *God to grow every tree that is pleasant to the sight, and good for food; the tree of life also in the midst of the garden, and the tree of knowledge of good and evil.*

The ancient Greeks had the Garden of the Hesperides in which grew the tree bearing golden apples which had been Gaea's[20] wedding gift to Hera. The practice of horticulture goes well back into the history of ancient Egypt and the Hanging Gardens of Babylon were one of the seven wonders of the world. In the Moslem world gardens of great beauty were constructed from Spain to Pakistan and India. They combined architecture, water and planting with great subtlety and charm. The Chinese and Japanese have also devoted superb artistry to the creation of gardens. Italy continued the traditions already established in republican and imperial Rome and England invented a kind of garden peculiarly suited to its own climate but imitated, often at great cost, in many other places. France excelled in grandeur of the formal garden and the genius of André Le Nôtre produced the gardens of Versailles as a setting for the Sun King and the centralized government of his country. This practice of setting the buildings of government in a garden was widely imitated, especially in America.

Ebenezer Howard, pioneer of modern town planning, conceived 'the garden city'[21] and it is of great significance that this idea was displaced by the geometrical *ville radieuse* of Le Corbusier and his concept of a human hive, the *Unité d'habitation*. It is even more revealing that nowadays private gardening has

brought the art of horticulture, on a small scale, to
levels never before achieved and by scientifically
guided sympathy with nature new varieties of flowers
and vegetables have been created. But the art of the
public garden has declined; few new parks are made
and we have become accustomed to pathetic attempts
at 'landscaping' the lonely bits of land severed from
their context by motorways. One of the reasons why
public gardens are not often made is that vandals, who
seem to be a product of the neurosis of our time, are
particularly inclined to loose their destructive urge
upon gardens. They symbolize, perhaps, what is missing in the stunted lives of juvenile delinquents
brought up in the concrete jungle of utilitarian
accommodation.

In literature the garden is a constant symbol, simile
or metaphor as with Shakespeare:

> *I am arrived from fruitful Lombardy*
> *The pleasant garden of great Italy.*

In a contrary sense he expresses Hamlet's despair:

> *How weary, stale, flat and unprofitable*
> *Seem to me all the uses of this world.*
> *Fie on't! O fie! 'tis an unweeded garden*
> *That grows to seed; things rank and gross in nature*
> *Possess it merely.*

Francis Bacon wrote;

> *God Almighty first planted a garden; and, indeed,*
> *it is the purest of human pleasures.*

The perfervid imagination of Coleridge conceived a synthesis of the classical garden with the horrific aspects of romanticism, in *Kubla Khan*;

> *So twice five miles of fertile ground*
> *With walls and towers were girded round:*
> *And here were gardens bright with sinuous rills,*
> *Where blossomed many an insence-bearing tree;*
> *And here were forests ancient as the hills,*
> *Enfolding sunny spots of greenery.*
> *But oh! that deep romantic chasm which slanted*
> *Down the green hill athwart a cedarn cover!*
> *A savage place! as holy and enchanted*
> *As e'er beneath a waning moon was haunted*
> *By woman wailing for her demon-lover.*

The intellectual Voltaire concluded his perceptive critique of optimism with the cryptic words:

> *Cela est bien dit, répondit Candide, mais il faut cultiver nôtre jardin.*

Nowadays, perhaps the idea of the unweeded garden possessed by 'things rank and gross in nature' is the most evocative, and like Hamlet we are paralysed by doubt, by uncertainty of our objectives in the face of usurped power. We know that the ghost walks the ramparts but our indecision, our clutching at false hopes, our half-faith in worn-out, irrelevant creeds prolongs the agony and brings disaster upon the innocent as well as upon the foolish.

To attack the massed batteries of weighty philosophy with a trowel and watering can may seem as

gross an impertinence as David confronting the
heavily armoured Goliath with a sling, but a great
deal of this philosophy belongs in truth to the lumber-
rooms of the mind. One might study Hegel, for
example, not because his philosophy is right but to
see how his ideas, utterly wrong though they must seem
to most modern people, take their place in the history
of human thought and have become embedded in
Marxism and in modern materialism (capitalist and
communist) which is destructive of the environment
and threatens the extinction of the human race by
drowning in its own effluent. As James Joll remarks,
'refuse disposal has always been one of the problems
confronting utopian thinkers',[22] and human ingenuity
has been envisaged as devising automatic means of
avoiding this chore. Nobody foresaw that refuse would
become a major limitation upon human progress and
Malthus was a lonely voice in pointing to the dangers
of human fertility. The great tide of nineteenth-
century political and social philosophy flowed on in
virtual ignorance of these important parameters.
Godwin was taking an extreme view when he wrote
in 1793

> *Perfectibility is one of the most unequivocal*
> *characteristics of the human species, so that the*
> *political as well as the intellectual state of man may*
> *be presumed to be in a course of progressive*
> *improvement.*[23]

But Godwin was by no means alone in his faith in the
progress of man without any natural restraints. He
was an idealistic anarchist whose ideas attracted a

great deal of ridicule but a surprising number of them are now tacitly accepted. There is, however, one great snag in idealistic anarchism, a snag which is apparent to the senses of anyone who has actual experience of the collapse of organization such as happens in the aftermath of war or revolution. It is simply the overwhelming smell of shit, and something has to be done about it. This necessary collaboration is the beginning of the end of anarchy and the first step towards new institutions.

With care, human excreta can be turned to beneficial use and the bacteria of decay make valuable manure for the soil. This is such a basic fact of life that the philosophers may be excused for ignoring it but the rapacious materialist societies of modern times create a great quantity of inorganic as well as a profusion of organic waste and this is a new problem.

Essentially the social-political-philosophical problems of our time are *different* because we are coming up against ecological boundaries beyond which exploitation will not merely show diminishing returns for effort but will produce a harmful reaction. Mankind has to go through the kind of experience which confronts the gilded youth whose father dies leaving him nothing but a mortgaged house full of shabby old furniture. He has to start afresh and come to terms with the world.

We may come back to the edifice of thought which we have inherited, for there must be a great deal of good in it, but we have the unprecedented problem, as a species, of being on or over the edge of the ecological balance. We have to create a new balance with nature and a consideration of how the gardener does this is not irrelevant. Unfortunately the great majority of city-dwellers know little or nothing about gardens.

A garden is an artificial ecological unit in which man works with and upon nature to achieve a pre-determined result. This is by no means easy, as every gardener knows. The difficulty is generally propor-tional to the degree of displacement from the natural ecological balance of the site. It is easier to grow blackberries in Scotland than peaches and mangoes flourish where it would be almost impossible to grow heather.

A garden begins with a piece of land which is marked off and, ideally, surrounded with walls. This land already has an ecology which has probably been influenced by man but the gardener plans to grow different plants and in so doing he alters the animal and insect communities related to the existing vegeta-tion. He starts by clearing the land and then prepares the soil. This is a long process and the quality of the soil will be changing and improving year by year if he does his work properly. The preparation of the soil involves the use of tools, which are products of industry but, apart from the tools, the bricks in the surrounding wall and chemicals such as insecticides and fertilizers, the gardener is working with his own hands and mind not to defy nature but, by creating the right conditions, by selection and manipulation, to work with nature in order that nature may do things she would not do on her own. Man, the gardener becomes an active participant in nature, a force in the garden without which it would go back to a more primitive ecology, but not to what it originally was because the soil has been altered and the old sequence broken. A neglected garden has an ecology of its own, the ecology of having been once directed by man. In some places nettles are the common heirs to man's habitation.

The use and character of a garden is something man decides. It may be a market garden producing vegetables and salad or it may be purely for pleasure and recreation, or it may be mainly for cut-flowers to be enjoyed elsewhere. Most gardens have a mixture of uses but it would be hard to find one which is so utilitarian that it contains no aesthetic element.

Into his prepared soil the gardener puts seeds and plants. These are not something which has been made from raw materials; they are alive and their history goes right back through millions of years of evolution. In recent times selective breeding and crossing have produced innumerable new varieties and there is no foreseeable end to the possibility of man guiding nature to produce better and better varieties. But here there is a danger. These new varieties are in a sense artificial and depend upon man as a partner in the ecological system. Remove man and most of them will perish or revert. Furthermore, the exotic varieties are sometimes more vulnerable and qualities such as perfume may be lost in developing bigger and brighter flowers. Man's value judgements come into this: if people want big roses of fine shape at the expense of perfume then horticulturists will select and breed to that end but if perfume in roses, for example, were given priority breeding would tend in that direction. One is working with a limited genetic structure which has its inherent limitations, checks and balances.

Climate is the most obviously powerful limiting factor in gardening but even this can be altered by enclosure with glass or other translucent material and artificial climates can be created but obviously at greater cost as they differ from the natural climate. The more exotic the artificial ecological community the more dependent it is upon the gardener.

Gardening has its own rules. These are not devised by gardeners. They are not morals nor are they an ethical system. They do not get expressed in such a form as 'Thou shalt not overwater young tomato plants in a cool greenhouse'. They simply say, 'if you overwater young tomato plants in a cool greenhouse they will probably damp off', i.e. rot at the neck, fall down and die. The 'morality' of the garden is of the *if you do this then that will happen* kind. It is empirical and based upon observation and experience. The question of what ought to happen is decided by the gardener on the basis of value judgements related to his knowledge of what is possible. Being a gardener he will think it is bad for plants to die and good for them to grow.

But it is not quite so simple as that. The gardener knows, and science is continually helping him to improve this knowledge, that values have to be weighed against each other and that certain procedures, for example, will give short-term results and lead to long-term failure. The most obvious case is that a plant may be forced to flower early but will be no use next year. If cost-effectiveness comes into the calculations maximum profitability may be set against high risk of crop failure or long-term disadvantages.

The vegetable garden exists mainly to provide food

but aesthetic considerations apply, not only in the design of the garden but in the quality of the produce and here there is usually a clash between cost-effectiveness and quality. For example it is easier to pick peas when the whole row can be done once and for all, but by that time many of the peas will be coarse. Selective picking as the pods ripen yields a much finer vegetable. That is to say a vegetable which tastes better. This is an aesthetic distinction. Many crops, such as carrots, are best when they have not reached maximum weight. It is true, of course, that young carrots may fetch a better price than old ones but suppose we argue that we ought, in a hungry world, to get the maximum yield from the soil, then we might argue that carrots should be harvested only when they are fully grown. 'Yes,' says the gardener, 'but there is a snag in that too. Leave them in the soil and they stand a greater risk of being damaged by pests.'

'Well use more pesticides.'

'Yes, but are you sure you are not poisoning the carrots and the people who will eat them and besides, pesticides may kill good as well as bad things in the soil.'

The gardener may well prefer good clean cultivation of a living soil to the interference and possible damage which chemicals may do to the ecological balance of his garden.

These are practical considerations. When we consider the pleasure-garden, clearly value judgements must be made on a different level. A hedonistic approach would be to say that the use of a pleasure-garden is to give pleasure, so that which gives most pleasure is best. But even apart from the doubt about who is to be pleased this is no answer. The garden is a work of art and the argument moves into the difficult field of aesthetics. The values to be taken into account are artistic values. The judgements to be made are akin to those made by painters, sculptors and poets but the gardener, as an artist, is working with living, not insensate materials.

The point is that value judgements are always difficult to make but they cannot be avoided. Decisions have to be made, such as to harvest early, selectively or late and they have to be based on value judgements. In the garden this is man's role, to make judgements, and he makes them in two different frames of reference. Firstly there is the garden itself and his intentions for it. If his intentions are clear then a good gardener can make these decisions easily, action being determined by his assessment of the relationship of his intentions, based upon practical and/or aesthetic considerations, to the observed and generally predictable performance of nature in his garden. The second frame of reference is much more difficult because it is the world outside, and this is chaotic. The gardener makes his decisions as best he can, but many decisions affecting him and his garden may be made without his knowledge and contrary to the interests of him and his garden. For example it may be decided to turn it into a parking place, an oily smelling dead patch of concrete instead of the living community he has fostered and cultivated. This may seem to him to be utterly wrong and being a gardener he may think, if he is also a philosopher, that if his garden were a model for the whole world there would be a universal frame of reference. His garden would be a garden within a garden. Who then would be the head gardener?

It is not a whimsical question. If we are to have an ecological morality it will involve the whole earth in the establishment of a balanced and beneficial participation of man in nature such as exists in a garden. And because the existence of a garden implies a gardener we shall have to answer the question.

I do not want to prolong the analogy with a garden to the length of a treatise on gardening. There are many of these. Our problem now is to consider the ethical implications of accepting the model of a garden, as being a beneficial accommodation with nature such as we must seek to achieve.

The garden is a useful analogy but not a pattern for human affairs. There is one major difference. A garden is a complex, controlled ecological system with a single administration, the gardener. True there may be numerous gardeners but in that case there is a head-gardener and a single policy. It would be fallacious to project this pattern to a world scale and argue that the whole surface of the earth should be treated as a single garden under the aegis of a head gardener. Gardening itself provides as good a reason as any why this is not acceptable: it would not work. There is a limit to the *size* of a garden. It is of its nature to be a limited enclosure of a size which can be comprehended. It is surrounded by land which is otherwise used, for farming or for habitations perhaps. Moreover, all gardens are different and each is a product of man's vision and effort in relation to the site. It is not unreasonable to say that each garden has a 'personality' in that it is a unique and sensitive organism which is in a continual

state of change and we rightly speak of an old garden
as being 'mature'. It has qualities which can only
occur with the passage of time. It would be a mistake
to blow up the microcosm of the garden into the
macrocosm of a world order but the *kind of thinking*
and the *value judgements* which belong to horticulture and with variations, and on a larger scale to
farming, ranching and forestry, are indicative of the
way in which we should proceed. The garden is the
most intimate and controlled participation of man in
an artificial ecological system, perhaps viticulture
comes next and then farming. Forestry is characterized by very long-term planning and ranching is nearer
to exploitation of the country, but the rancher over-
stocks and over-grazes at the peril of creating a dust-
bowl. To survive he must be acutely aware of the
balance between cattle and grass. The nomad, on the
other hand, moves on and like the primitive kind of
hunter embodies the rapacious mind, the exploitative
attitudes of modern materialism.

And before we pass on it may be noted that, like
the garden, the industrial plant becomes a self-contained organism exploiting not only natural resources
but labour, that is, man himself. Thus an industry
is attracted to an area where there is surplus female
labour which can be drawn away from home and
children. A new social pattern is established around
the plant, a purely man-machine relationship which
ignores the rest of nature and all values outside itself
except profitability or cost-effectiveness. If social
justification is required then the demand for the
product is held to provide this justification. The effect
on the human community may be judged good or bad

according to differing scales of value (human dignity versus productivity for example) but the relationship with nature, is terrible. Whereas one can contemplate with pleasure the notion of the earth cultivated as innumerable gardens wherever site and climate permit gardens to be, the proliferation of ecologically un-integrated industrial communities everywhere it is possible to put factories and housing would be horrible. Imagine Birmingham extending like a vast scab over the whole land-surface of the earth!

It is useless and silly to pretend that we can do without industry[24] but it cannot be paramount. It must take its place in a controlled ecology which takes account of a great many other values.

Chapter Five

Man and the Environment

greedy/extortionate

The rapacious society is destructive of an environment of which man is a part. Ecological morality can only be based upon a balance with nature which is beneficial to man, but we must assert quality of living over against conventional economic values. The implications are global, local and personal.

Global considerations relate to man as such. He is a single species with an enormous and advantageous capacity for variation and adaptation. Cultivation of variety can lead to the development of man whereas egalitarianism is repressive. Cultivation depends upon true knowledge. Men need to collaborate and no ecosystem* can be self-sufficient.

Local considerations involve the cells which make up the total organism. This totality cannot be defined because it is in a constant state of growth from within. The local ecosystems and the individuals within them have a contributory and creative relationship to the whole instead of a predatory one. Ecosystems must not be too large and the reason for present power-groupings are seen to belong to the rapacious society and to have no ecological validity. Each locality is unique but all are inter-dependent. Freedom within

* *Ecosystem*: A community of organisms interacting with one another, plus the environment in which they live and with which they also interact. (*Penguin Dictionary of Biology*)

an ecosystem is freedom to participate and implies liabilities. Services common to groups of ecosystems will have to be worked out. Man has to live *with* not against nature, the health of each cell being important to the health of the whole organism at local level and globally.

THE ANALOGY with a garden has indicated the kind of thinking which may be applied to our problem of improving the human condition while reversing the very means by which man has, for more than a hundred years, sought to combat poverty by increasing wealth and short-term exploitation of the natural riches of Earth. Most of the world is still desperately poor but we cannot contemplate the extension of rapacious industrialism.[25] As we noted at the beginning of the last chapter, a political solution cannot be expected from political systems which rest upon a foundation of exploitative materialism, but it would be idle to suppose that the development of a new world order based upon a new morality involving new evaluations and leading, we believe, to a higher quality of life, is going to come into being spontaneously. The garden implies a gardener. It does not happen, it is made by conscious effort often in the face of great difficulty. It requires perseverance and an element of ruthlessness based upon clear decisions. One garden cannot be every kind of garden and no garden can tolerate the free growth of weeds. The purpose of this book is to formulate the bases of a new morality but the way of thinking which we are adopting firmly excludes *laissez-faire*. It is not the purpose of this book to resuscitate liberalism. On the contrary, the principal hope for the implementation of the new outlook on life must rest upon the adaptation of institutions and procedures which have been worked out by socialists.[26] Obviously we cannot look to capitalism for the balanced order which we require, but neither can we look to socialism in its present form because it is still obsessed by economic considerations in relation to man alone and without respect to the rest of nature.

We have also reached another parting of the ways. A world order can either be thought of as imposed or as coming into existence through collaboration. H. G. Wells, in *The Shape of Things to Come*[27] foresaw the collapse of civilization and reversion to barbarism from which mankind was rescued by the initiative of a small group of supermen, but Wells envisaged mankind surviving without genetic damage. They were healthy barbarians. The collapse of civilization through competitive war is, as Wells foresaw, quite possible but the hazard is now much more dangerous, and the possibility of rescue more remote.

We have to achieve a new world order and there is an obvious temptation, which underlies the political thinking of at least two great powers, to believe that this order can be imposed by force, that one group can become 'world-gardener'. This is a practical impossibility even if it were morally acceptable which, in terms of our thinking in this book, it is not. The new weapons have not abolished the balance of power so beloved of nineteenth-century political theorists but have created a new and much more majestic balance over against nature, the inevitable recoil upon the users of power. But quite apart from the impossibility of successful war, the other challenge with which we have been concerned throughout this book cannot be solved by force. There are those who say that excessive populations should be wiped out and argue that the more advanced races need to take this kind of action, that we should spray swarming men like swarming locusts. One has only to consider the moral recoil in U.S.A. from the bombing of Hiroshima and Nagasaki, and the war in Vietnam, to realize that such a policy could not be successfully pursued. It is a political and moral impossibility and it is politically impossible for moral reasons, no matter how unreasonable these may seem to some people.

But merely to eliminate excessive populations would not touch the central problem. The increase would recur and the pruning would have to be done again. It is inconceivable that the over-all power would remain intact. It would be the target for every ambitious group and would create a chronic state of competitive violence.

Man must not contemplate the establishment of an omnipotent authority. This is a chimera, but there is abundant evidence that large-scale co-operatives can be achieved and can work. What we need is a powerful consensus of opinion and agreement about objectives based upon a moral foundation which commands both respect and belief.

Fundamentally the need is to abandon the nine-teenth-century grand-design approach, which has the attraction of simplicity, and substitute an awareness of mankind as necessarily a participant in nature which has its own laws. Man has a great deal of scope for adapting and manipulating these laws but he

cannot escape or override them. Instead of the grand-
design, the idealistic philosophy which embraced
earth and sometimes heaven as well,[28] we have the
fact of innumerable related organisms. We have to
learn to think about relationships and to understand
that nothing is isolated or simple. We must not
expect to find and be guided by a simple formulation
of principles in the detailed conduct of our lives and
the organization of our social groups. But an overall
concept is possible. We can be aware of the totality
of nature as an infinitude of components all inter-
related. Within this totality we can manoeuvre to
achieve a beneficial balance.

The complexity and fluidity of our problems
exclude the possibility of a simple rational argument.
Unfortunately we have reached a stage in human
intellectual development where many thoughtful
people expect, and have been conditioned by their
education to expect, straightforward arguments leading to firm conclusions; but in modern science and
philosophy, while such mental processes are valid at
the lower levels, they have been modified on the
frontiers of thought. *Whenever we proceed from the
known into the unknown we may hope to understand,
but we may have to learn at the same time a new
meaning of the word 'understanding'.*[29] We are
moving away from doctrine, which requires uncom-
promising belief, towards an openness to the
immensity of what we do not know. Our present
attempt to develop new moral attitudes must be an
exploration, rather than an argument towards a
doctrinal conclusion, and we begin with a number of
considerations which may be relevant. Some refine-

ment of these will be attempted later. For the moment they appear as a collection of thoughts, ideas, facts and observations.

We may conceive an ecological morality as being a way to cultivate and maintain a beneficial balance of nature, including man as a part of nature. Man being what he is, it would be unrealistic to regard the 'benefit' as being anything but 'beneficial to man'; but the rapacious society has exemplified the fact that in asserting his own rights to benefit he must respect the rest of nature. If he does not do so he himself loses thereby. It would be possible to argue that man should love and respect nature for its own sake, out of charity so to speak, and if necessary at cost to himself. But such an argument would have to be based upon a prior commitment to love of nature analogous to the Christian commitment to love of mankind. It would be essentially a religious argument and this is to be avoided for the practical reason that it would have to compete with all other religious arguments and faiths. It may, in the judgement of some people, be a meaner thing to base our new morality upon practical necessity and benefit to man, but this does not exclude what they may regard as higher motives. The advantage is that ecological morality can compete with the economic concept of man on its own terms. The principal enemy is economic materialism rather than religions which, having their roots in pre-materialistic times, when man was a relatively frail component in the ecological balance, could probably accept an ecological morality without strain though there would be some important exceptions such as the Roman Catholic prejudice against birth control.

In opposing the ecological view of man to the economic we are, in effect, asserting the importance of quality of living over against money. At the common-sense level most people are aware that 'you can't buy happiness or health'. Materialist society has committed itself to money which cannot buy what we need and desire. If we re-shape our thinking and accept an ecological morality economics will not disappear as a subject of thought, and as a necessary discipline in administration, but its objectives will be altered to take account of new concepts of *value*. These must involve a better understanding of the nature of man.[30]

Man is a single species. Men are not all equal; on the contrary they are extremely diverse in talents, inheritance and aptitudes. This variety is character-istic of the species and constitutes one of its greatest strengths.

Man is a social animal and lives in communities. The work of these communities is divided and apportioned among men according to aptitude, train-ing, inheritance or custom. By having a defined role in society each individual may cultivate his ability in that role so that it is better performed, to the advan-tage of the community. This specialization of function has its dangers but it enables man to achieve far more than he would if everyone were a 'jack of all trades'.[31]

Man is a remarkably adaptable animal. The range of adaptation of the individual to environment is very great, as compared with other species, but over and above this, communities have acquired a collective adaptation to the conditions in which they have existed over long periods of time. Environment has favoured different genetic variations in different localities; thus, adaptation to environment is reflected in physical variations. For example dark skin colouring has advantages in tropical climates, compact physique in steep mountain districts and short strong legs where people cultivate rice.

Man is capable of increasing his range of adaptation by the application of knowledge and skill. An extreme example is his ability to get to the moon and walk about there. On Earth the creation of artificial climates is feasible. From very early times men have provided shade, warmth and air movement but now it is conceivable that whole communities could thrive in artificial climates.[32]

In the past human communities have been competitive, sometimes to the point where one exterminates or enslaves another. The instrument of such competition has been warfare. Whatever the arguments for and against war in the past may be, man has now reached a stage of development when war is as damaging to the aggressor as to the victim. It is no longer an effective activity and it threatens the existence of all life on Earth. Man has not yet outgrown war emotionally and it exerts a fascination for him like a flame has for a moth. Throughout nature there is violence but man's claim to supremacy requires him to reject violence between men. The human race is one and only weakens itself by strife.

The Earth is finite. Its resources are limited, distributed unevenly and many of them are inter-related. Air and ocean currents pay no heed to national boundaries and many biological phenomena, such as bird migrations and the spread of virus infections, are global, not local. The availability of natural resources such as minerals is the common concern of mankind. So also is the avoidance of waste.

Differences of philosophy, custom, language, organization and religion between communities are variations which enrich the totality of human experience, just as variety of talent and skill in individuals enriches social communities.

There is a limit to the number of human beings that can live on Earth. This can only be defined in terms of quality of living because, long before the physical limit of space available had been reached, man would have completely upset the ecological balance and become an infestation. The problem of population is of global concern to all men but the solution of the problem must come down to communities and individuals. It would be of little use to define an optimum world population regardless of its distribution.[33]

The cultivation of a balance in nature depends upon true knowledge of nature. Advancement of science, particularly the life-sciences, is of concern to all mankind; so is the communication and dissemination of knowledge, not only among 'advanced' peoples but also at primitive levels of society. Just as some communities have minerals and others can grow citrus fruits so a few communities have developed education in such a way as to facilitate intellectual excellence. Knowledge and high-thinking are a part of the ecological world-balance just as minerals and fruit crops are.

Apart from the need to reject war, the development of trade and technology, based upon science, has made human communities much more dependent

upon each other. Men have far more to gain by co-
operation than by disagreement. Attempts to impose
the ideas or will of one group upon another are
reactionary. They can only lead to strife, regression
and possible disaster.

Ecological communities are not self-contained. For
example a small island may seem to be very nearly
self-contained yet migrant and visiting birds give it
outside relations. If man comes into the picture, global
relationships are inevitable. Every locality is part of
the whole. This is the natural world order as opposed
to the political philosophers' and revolutionaries'
dreams of *imposing* a world order. The order is there
to be *found* and understood, not to be imposed by
blundering humans.

The world order is not something to be conceived
and imposed like the will of an architect. We are not
working with inanimate bricks and concrete but with
living communities of living species. The order must
be organic, not finite but growing. Instead of the
dreary concept of the world state, brought about by
the 'inexorable forces' of history helped on by the
violence of revolution to a fixed, hive-like economy
battening upon the rest of nature until man has so
fouled his nest that it is unbearable, we have an
infinite prospect of variation, growth and improvement. But growth and improvement must not be
thought of in the old mechanistic sense of 'progress'.
Rather we must consider the principle of complementarity whereby any variation in the environment
(including man) reflects back upon its cause. Thus,
most importantly for our present consideration, man,
as he cultivates the environment, will change himself

and his evaluations. Man is, by nature, an improving animal,[34] and the constant complementary inter-actions of change and evaluation provide infinite scope for continual reassessment of the nature of improvement. We cannot predict the course of change and 'improvement' but we can, again, believe in its possibility.

We cannot map the whole organism because it is growing from within. Our thinking has to be cellular. We 'cultivate our gardens' in the context of a world order which we cannot predetermine because it is a growing, changing, organic complex with which our 'garden', our ecological locality, has a complementary relationship.

What then is an ecological locality? If we were talking of ants or bees we might say it was limited to the maximum range of food gathering, but with migrant birds it would be much more difficult to define. Modern man has to be aware of a world ecology which is too big and complex for him to control according to any preconceived plan but of which he is a contributory part. The important thing seems to be that each component human community should at least be in balance; but reverting to the analogy of the garden, it would be a poor garden that yielded no increase and each ecological community ought to be able to enrich rather than impoverish the world. This implies a contributory or creative relationship to the whole rather than a predatory or exploitative one as at present.

An ecological locality, like a garden, is a cultivable unit. Clearly it will not be marked out to arbitrary dimensions and will vary according to the terrain and to the character and traditions of the people, but generally the modern nation-state would seem to be too large. What we think of as a region is more suitable for creating a community of people of such size that all can feel they are responsible participants. The city state has a splendid record of social, intellectual and artistic achievement but in a predatory society it was not strong enough. In the modern world we have super-states which are clearly not ecological units and would fall apart but for the over-riding considerations of power politics. We have nation states which were once big enough to be significant in the power game but are now too small to be effective 'powers' and too large to be ecological units. We have some small countries whose record is exemplary.[35]

The continuing reasons for the existence of 'great powers' are the rapacious society, the acceptance of war as a possibility and the economic advantages of large scale operation. Taking these in order: the rapacious society is destroying itself by its peoples' lack of faith in it, by the poor quality of living which it provides and by progressive exhaustion of resources; war must be rejected if men are to survive; and industry, far from being satisfied with national markets, even within the super-states, seeks maximum economic efficiency in world markets and supranational organizations.[36] If appeal is made to tradition and patriotism the *real* feelings of innumerable groups of people centre on much smaller regions than the nations of which they are parts at present. Britain for example would divide, probably into Scotland, North and South Wales, Ireland, and something like the Anglo-Saxon kingdoms. France has its natural and

historic provinces. Germany, until the nineteenth
century, was a linguistic group of small states which
achieved high standards of civilization. Russia is a
major imperialist power holding together former
nation states some of which, if they were free to do
so, would break up, not into the national groupings
they assumed in the age of nationalism but into
smaller units. The possible brilliance of human
achievement if all these peoples could be free to
develop according to their own genius, and not under
an overlordship for the sake of power, is immense.
The United States is much more significant as a
federation for mutual advantage than as what it has
recently become, a 'world power' manufacturing by
propaganda a spurious patriotic unity. Throughout
the world there are identifiable communities most of
which are submerged in the interests of a more powerful unity.

There are excellent reasons for believing that small
states are best for achieving quality of living but in
the face of war and economic war they are too vulnerable to survive except for reasons of convenience to
the great powers. These conditions are passing away
and we are left with one group of people who have a
strong vested interest in the power game. These are
the professional ambitious politicians who seek by
political means to achieve the eminence which once
accrued to military conquerors. These men have
already subjugated the generals, because military
organizations in the modern world are dependent
upon political masters who alone can supply them
with men and munitions. Among career politicians
the idea of largely self-governing ecological localities

is bound, because of self-interest, to be disliked and resisted by the usual means. But devolution of government to smaller units offers a great deal more opportunity for politicians of a different kind, because politicians do perform a necessary function in society. Furthermore the break-down of super-states will create a need for new networks of relationships. Some interesting prototypes for them already exist in the United Nations, international industrial and commercial organizations, air lines and supra-national bodies such as the European Common Market and the Supreme Council of the Soviets. An ecological basis for society will require a great variety of political and negotiatory skills in relating localities to each other and to the whole. This function is analagous to the way enzymes work as messengers or catalysts in living bodies.[37]

The first, and major political problem in establishing a world ecology is to break down the large social-political units into ecological localities. If this is seen as a desirable and necessary development in human affairs it will be achieved in some, the truly most progressive countries.[38] The obvious advantages in quality of life and opportunity as compared with the massive organizations will be the best argument for extension of the practice. But time is short and the longer we delay the more damage will have been done by the rapacious societies of the present time.

What are the implications of ecological morality within the localities?

Each locality is unique, in geography, in climate, in history, in techniques, in customs, in genetic composition.

All localities are interdependent, each contributing, according to its capacity and inclination, to the totality of existence on Earth. Each has to work out its own system of cultivation within the overall concept of ecological balance.[39]

A great deal of study needs to be given to the problem of creating a beneficial ecological balance. This is truly a new start in human affairs and should be an enormous and exciting challenge.[40]

While each locality must be free to work out its own system of cultivation such freedom necessarily implies certain responsibilities and restrictions which, if neglected, will have to be imposed by some form of collective organization. (More of this later.) Every citizen must have a sense of responsibility for his own locality, a feeling of involvement and a right to be there. There should be freedom of movement all over the Earth but there could not be unlimited right of settlement. It looks as though the ecological sub-divisions, the localities, will have to be based upon existing population distribution, though special provision would have to be made for immigration to underpopulated areas. As a general principle, however, people are part of the ecology and must make the most of what they are where they are. Thus if a community allows its population to grow it must accept, within itself, the responsibility for the effects the increase will have upon the quality of living. Furthermore, it seems inevitable that communities should be responsible for their governments. This is an essential principle. Freedom is not a one-way ticket. If each human being in a community has the right to participate in its government it is also his *responsibility* to participate and he must share in the collective responsibility of his government as a component in the world ecology. Thus if a local community has to be disciplined for infringement of the ecological rights of others the counterpart of freedom to participate in government is liability to correction. The higher authority[41] should only intervene in the internal affairs of a locality to protect the ecological rights of other localities.

Chapter Six

Ecological Morality and the Individual

We have religious and social moralities. Ecological morality is a third-level morality which derives from the nature of man and his environment. Where necessary it must override the moralities of religious or social groups. Its basis is awareness of the world as an organism in which all the living parts contribute to the whole. Within this concept the current difficulties of self in relation to society can be resolved because the health of the whole requires the cultivation of the parts.

There is no overall design. We are in a state of becoming. Freedom from oppression is the prerequisite of freedom to contribute and any healthy organization is a free association of individuals. The communality should be a sum of excellencies not of stunted growths due to repression.

Sound cultivation depends upon realistic assessment of potentialities. It is not for the new morality to define correct modes of behaviour for all men, in all places, at all stages of social development but to create the conditions in which human life may be enriched by innumerable contributions.

We are moving towards ecological morality in the growth of respect for minorities. The essence, for the individual, is that he should be *a participant not a subject*. Sexual responsibility is required in the context of the population explosion and we find greater understanding of this than awareness of the obscenity of violence. Each individual also has the environment of his own physique and personality the health of which requires cultivation.

WE ARE ACCUSTOMED to think of morality at two levels, the religious and the social. Sometimes these converge and social custom is equated with the law of God. A great many people, all around the world, believe in a god or gods and associated spiritual powers. They are perfectly entitled to do so. They are certainly not to be weaned from their beliefs by force.

Social morals are the customs of a community and are generally necessary to its communal life. They are not immutable, and some of them may be absurd, but usually people like the customs they have grown up with. People are generally sensible about their social customs. They like visitors to respect them but when they go abroad they expect to conform with the reasonable customs of other people while they are among them. The adherents of some religions are equally sensible but others have a bad record of intolerance. The worst are those who deny that they are intolerant because they 'know' they are 'right'. Ecological morality is a third level which does not exclude the other levels but may need to override them.

The basis of ecological morality is awareness of the world as an organism in which all the living parts contribute to the whole. It cannot accept invasive cells of malignant tissue without weakening and

threatening, the health of the whole organism. The
imposition of the social or religious morality of one
cell upon another would be such an invasion. We
have a right to cultivate our own garden, not our
neighbour's. If we cultivate our garden in such a way
as to endanger the ecology of our neighbour's garden
he has moral grounds to complain. Polluting his water
supply or poisoning his bees would be examples. As
with so many other matters which we have considered,
mankind is moving towards a third-level morality in
the growth of international law and already some of
the most difficult problems of international law concern ecological disputes such as oil pollution of coasts,
fishing grounds, disposal of waste and preservation of
wild life.

On the surface, third-level morality has so far made
little impact upon personal morality, but if we look
deeper, most of the honest demonstrations[42] are, in
fact concerned with the neglect of what young people
feel or intuit to be violations of what ought to be
international law. Instinct is again ahead of formulation.

But at the present time there is a split in moral
attitudes. On the one hand there is a growing sense
of social responsibility. There has never been a time
when more people, especially young people, have cared
so much and so actively about mankind as a whole
yet, in many parts of the world people believe, and
are taught to believe, that self-realization is supremely
important. Enlightened educationists proceed in the
faith that they should seek to develop the potential
of every child so that it may grow up to be as rounded
and self-realized a personality as possible.[43] Such

educationists frequently have a strong social sense and believe that it is for the good of the community that people should be educated to make the most of themselves, but liberal minded socialists find themselves in stark ideological conflict with those who believe that the state is a collective human entity to which individual personalities and aspirations must be subordinate and for which, if necessary, they must be sacrificed. Moreover, young people emerge from an educational system which has encouraged their individuality, to find themselves committed to social organizations which strictly limit their activities, and demand, often on pain of loss of 'the right to work', the subjugation of individuality. The socialist state may be seen as the trade union writ large and its sad paradox for the activist who is working towards the establishment of socialist states is that, when he succeeds, there will be no place for people like him. Many young people are acutely aware of the contradiction between liberal education and the kind of society towards which supposedly avant garde thought is leading us. Hence much frustration, despair and tacit acceptance of the coming of Orwell's *1984*, whatever political route we take. The trouble arises from our so-called progressive thinking being still bounded by mid-nineteenth-century knowledge and ways of thought. There is, as we have already noted (p. 3) every excuse for this because social reform on traditional communist lines seems to be so desperately necessary in many countries where nineteenth-century conditions exist in a form exacerbated by modern technology. What Marx took for the light at the end of the tunnel was, however, merely a miner's lantern, and there is still a long way

to go to the daylight and fresh air of the ecological
society.

Much might be said about the conflict between the
individual and society but I shall not pursue this line
of thought because in ecological morality the conflict
can be resolved.

Man made the state in his own primitive image. In
place of a father-figure he put the human master. The
socialist state is the creation of an exploited proletariat
which gets rid of the master—the capitalists—only to
make itself *master* of itself. For this morbid image we
have to substitute awareness of the living totality
which the modern life-sciences have disclosed. Man is
not separate and no human organization can, in the
nature of things, be supreme. We are part of an
organic whole and any organization which we may
construct for ourselves has to fit into that whole, not
as a mechanical part but as a living cell. Here we may
be reminded of a very old fable, *The Belly and the
Members*. All the parts of a body are interdependent.
Even the mind is not something separate and located
in the brain. We know, for example, that the action
of the brain is affected by glands in other parts of the
body, and an interesting way in which new knowledge
has liberated us from old thought patterns is that we
no longer need to think of sexual activity as being
distinctively 'carnal'. In the mid-nineteenth century
such a separation of mind and body was an obvious
conclusion from what appeared to be the facts. Our
thinking about sex is at once more simple, in that we
see it as part of the whole person, and more complicated in that we recognize, though we do not yet fully
understand, the existence of an infinitude of comple-

mentary relationships within the individual and be-tween participants in sexual attraction and activity. It should cause no surprise that the process whereby life is extended provides a better model of the way the world works than the man-made systems based upon inadequate and often incorrect information.

Our own modern knowledge is also incomplete but the evidence now indicates that there is no overall plan, no blueprint for the universe with man as the chief executive. On the contrary, nature builds up from simple to more complex organisms and among the social animals, such as man, from individual to mating, to family, to tribe and so on. It is always growth upwards and outwards. Man, it is true, has some limited power to manipulate this growth, as he does when he makes a mushroom bed, but in all his cultivation he takes an existing condition and develops it, from seed or cutting, offset or layering to a new mature plant, and when he begins to breed new varieties he does so by crossing and selection not know-ing what the new variety will be, what characteristics it will have, whether it will be hardy or delicate. But by observation and understanding of the workings of genetics and the laws of probability he may have some idea of the way in which he is going. He may even have a preconception of what he wants to breed; a fast racehorse or a blue rose but he cannot *design* these in the sense that an engineer designs a bridge. For two hundred years we have been obsessed by the idea of *design* both as an active process, as in designing a machine, and as a metaphysical idea, based upon analogy with the active process, whereby we conceive the world to have been *designed*. And if we are reli-

giously inclined we may say God was the designer (and
dodge the question of who designed God). What is
being revealed by science is hard to explain or understand in terms of the old mental models. The organic
part of nature is in a constant state of growth, fertile
decay and regeneration. This occurs on the basis of
what we distinguish as inanimate matter which we
conceive to be the building material out of which
living things are fashioned. Whether this is a satisfactory analogue may be doubted but here we are concerned with living things and particularly with man.
He is a self-conscious, growing and changing organism
which, though it has a temporary distinct existence,
does so only in the context of a larger organism which
itself is not static. Our lives are properly to be
described as a *state of being*, defined at both ends by
a *state of not being in that state* though all the components 'exist' before, during and after, not at any
time in a fixed state but in a flux of relationships.
The mind boggles at this multidimensional infinitude
of relationships and we have to make small models to
think with, but these now have to be biologically
consistent with the whole which is not a design but
a growing organism. The easiest analogy for us now
is the cell, living and participating, dependent but
distinct.

But we are more than cells in the ordinary biological
sense. In thinking of ourselves in that way we are
using the simple to explain the complex. Cells norm-
ally reproduce themselves identically but man, like
other animals, is unique. The process of heredity in
such a complex organism as man creates a unique
individual each time (identical twins are an exception

but they are quickly differentiated by environment). The human community builds up out of the association of individuals each making his own contribution. But like any other animal, man can be subjugated, caged, exploited by men. The question of freedom has concerned us for many centuries but until recently, almost always in negative terms. That is to say man has wanted freedom from restraint because there was obvious oppression and exploitation everywhere. But a positive attitude to freedom has been developed, particularly by modern educationists, whereby freedom is seen firstly as freedom to 'be oneself' (and not the creature of someone else, moulded to his desires) and secondly, as a free individual to make one's contribution to the social organism. Freedom from oppression is the pre-requisite of freedom to give of one's best and this is the true freedom. Thus, in an ecological morality the relationship of the individual to society is one of involvement not of compulsion, of contribution not of required labour.

This is basic. Any healthy social organization is a free association of individuals. It is created by them for their convenience and has no existence in its own right. Resting upon this basis, ecological morality requires of the individual that he be the best that he can be so that the sum of individual contributions to the communality should be a sum of excellencies rather than of stunted growths, unrealized potentialities and deficiences. There is certainly a sense in which the whole is more than the sum of its parts but the sum will be greater or less according to the *quality* of the parts and it must be remembered that each social 'whole' is itself a part of a greater whole, and so on to

infinity, because even if there are bounds in space as
ordinarily understood, the relationship with time
takes it beyond our powers of conception.

It is asserted as a cardinal moral principle that each
individual should be free to make the best contribution he can to the society in which he participates.
This raises a host of questions, not so much of
principle but of practicality. Men are not islands,
they are more like blades of grass in a field—thousands
upon thousands of them, each limited but also
supported by the others around him. In most human
activities there is no problem of one man's contribution excluding another's. In the ordinary tasks of
cooking, carpentry, bricklaying, nursing, dentistry,
teaching and so on it is in everyone's interest that
each should do the best of which he is capable but
this does create certain natural restraints. Those who
do their job better will tend to frustrate those who
do the same job less well. People will seldom prefer
badly cooked food to good meals but the humble
aspirant to fulfil himself as a chef is inhibited if he
has no ability in that direction. Thus there must
clearly be an environmental component in fulfilling
oneself. Ecological morality must be realistic as nature
is, favouring the healthy against the sickly and, it
must be said, the strong in any particular activity
against the weak. The problem is of everyday
familiarity to most teachers, in that a child's education must be related to his capacity, having regard to
the environment in which that capacity will be
deployed. It is a problem of cultivation, of producing
a healthy growth, neither forced nor stunted. Ecologi-

cal morality cannot accept an egalitarianism, such as we apply when we mow the lawn, which restricts the development of the exceptional talent. A pine tree has as much right not to be stunted as has the gorse bush or the hawthorn.

It is possible to imagine an ideal state in which all men were filled with goodwill, and each, with a combination of zeal and perfect tact, made the best possible contribution from himself to the communal existence. For practical purposes we can forget this excursion of the imagination. We are imperfect people with a long history of discord, wickedness and disease behind us. Some of us are born maimed either mentally or physically and our capacities and talents vary widely. We are subjected from birth to many influences which may warp our character. All kinds of accidents may occur and our responses to these may embitter or enlighten us. Our minds are far from perfect and the opportunities for cultivating them are erratic. We have intense problems within us and few are entirely without greed, cruelty and weakness. We are all a mixture of what we call good and bad but we have only the vaguest notions of what we really mean by good and bad. We used to be fairly sure there were absolute standards but now they appear to be more circumstantial and relative. This creates difficulties which, in our general laziness, make us 'permissive' in the sense that we don't bother.

We have to consider man as he is, not perfect nor perfectible but capable of living at various levels of quality from squalid brutality upwards, apparently without limit. We cannot foretell what man may become but we do find that cultivation leads to improve-

ment. For centuries man has limped forward, with
many setbacks. Most of these have been caused by
conflict between groups of men. Such conflict has been
rooted in competition to survive in a hostile environment, to trade rivalry, to differences in religious faith
and latterly, and most deadly, to ideological disagree-
ments. Men have cherished their excuses for division
and they still do, for selfish motives, even if those
selfish motives are idealized in the form of 'what they
believe in'. The fact that someone believes in something is, in itself, no excuse for anything, least of all
hostility to fellow men.

Within the context of a complex, divided and very
far from perfect human race, the scope of ecological
morality is not to define correct modes of behaviour
for all men in all places and at all stages of social
development. This would be entirely contrary to the
ecological concept of balanced growth. We must not
seek to achieve perfection along one road but should,
on the contrary, endeavour to create the conditions in
which human life may be enriched by innumerable
different contributions. The analogy may be with flow-
ering plants. The basic 'idea' of such a plant is that it
produces flowers which attract pollinating insects so
that fertile seeds are produced. The common daisy
is as good an example as any. It is efficient, hardy and
compact. Why should nature bother to have other
kinds of flowers in a locality which is suited to daisies?
The daisy species may be compared to a single social-
moral system. There is no need to labour the point
that a great deal would be lost if we only had daisies.[44]

But what about the predatory aspect of nature? It
is extremely highly developed in man and in the past

peaceful and admirable communities have been destroyed or enslaved by people who excelled only in strength and brutality. Whole civilizations have disappeared under the impact of 'barbarians'. And among modern so-called civilized nations hideous wars have been fought because of different ideas about how society should be organized and for various other competitive reasons. But in the last half century man has passed an important crisis in evolution. He has extended the technique of war to its logical conclusion, foreshadowed by Clausewitz,[45] of total war. Our generation has perfected the means and is in process of realizing that total war equals total destruction. Since nobody can be expected to fight war within the rules of a game all war is potentially total war and total destruction, not merely of a civilization but of all higher forms of life on Earth. This is absurd. The predatory principle of man killing man will not do. It is bound to take time for human beings to adjust their ideas, thoughts, values and prejudices, and even their forms of entertainment, to the conditions which have been created by the application of science to the technique of war. It is essential that the peace should be kept and Vietnam has been the crucible in which many old ideas have been melted.

But a new and infinitely important belief is gaining a hold over the minds of men and is evidenced in such things as legislation against racial discrimination. Such legislation was conceivable but politically impossible in Britain or US.A. fifty years ago. There is a growing awareness of the need to recognize the right of all people to live in their own way and develop without predatory interference. There are three

principal dangers. There are the political 'do-gooders'
who want to go around weeding other people's gardens
without knowing weeds from wistaria.[46] There are
the great powers which use weak communities as
pawns in the power game. There are industrial
empires which have reasons for holding back or im-
poverishing underdeveloped areas. There is a world-
wide conflict of interest between the rapacious high-
standard of living industrial community and the
primary producers of food and raw materials. There
used to be a sane balance between town and country
but in the industrially advanced countries this has
been lost[47] and the dichotomy is world wide.

Short-term self-interest, which is highly motiva-
tional, especially in democratic countries, exacerbates
this fatal division but even so there is more than lip-
service, indeed there is a growing weight of respect
for the rights of minorities as more and more people
realize that they themselves are, in one way or another,
members of minorities. Close associations of groups
for self-protection are typical, from trade and professional unions and societies to consumer associations,
parents associations, protest marches, and a host of
other group activities which represent minority
opinions and interests in what seems to be an increasingly monolithic and impersonal system. Selfishness
may not be the most admirable of motives but the
confluence of self-interest with the philosophical concept of *self*, aided by modern psychological research,
is producing a powerful undercurrent of dislike for
the monolithic state in particular countries and sheer
horror at the prospect of its world-wide extension.

It makes all the difference whether we consider 'the

whole' to be *divided* into constituent units which are individuals or whether we consider 'the whole' to be the product of its parts, which are individuals. In the last hundred and fifty years science has been moving away from the concept of a given amount of matter which was, according to Newtonian physics, depreciating, to new ideas heralded by the concept of the expanding universe, by such ideas as continuous creation and then such notions as matter and antimatter which would have seemed like mysticism a century ago.[48] Perhaps the change may be most simply summarized as being the recognition that infinity is a 'reality' and not just a mathematical symbol. Being aware of the infinitude of the universe a 'totality' of organized humanity being like an ant hill in minor orbit round a minor star, looks absurd. With the philosophical stuffing taken out of it the world state as an actual power in its own right over all men appears to be a moth-eaten sham and our modern knowledge of the biological sciences reveals an infinitude of replicating organisms. It would be literally monstrous to conceive the 'whole of nature' as a vast body subdivided into organic parts! We have to see it as an *ecosystem* which is defined as *a community of organisms, interacting with one another, plus the environment in which they live and with which they also interact.*[49] One has only to study any pond, wood, field or cultivated garden to see that the *community* is not a state with power. It is a totality of individuals. And in a garden, where man intervenes he does not do so with complete authority but only as a powerful influence in the ecology, as a *participant* not as a summation comprising everything within his selfhood.

So, for the individual, the implication of an ecological morality is that he should be a participant, not a subject.

In this context personal morality becomes a matter of responsible participation and as such might have to override certain religious and social moral precepts. Morals should grow and mutate according to the conditions of the environment and should not be limited and defined 'for all time' by a theoretical code. There will be no attempt here to consider particular moral systems in an ecological context because this is a vast work which must be done by many minds in many places, but attention should perhaps be drawn to the fundamentality of sex because it is the means whereby life is continued. This is obviously the primary role of sex and for human beings the problems of living with a powerful sex urge are secondary to this. The inherent quality of offspring is largely dependent upon heredity and it is well known that certain diseases, which affect heredity, can produce offspring which are maimed physically and mentally. On the other hand selective breeding can improve a stock and the human species is not exempt from this simple fact. One cannot escape the conclusion that ecologically any and every human community will be affected in its communal well-being by its sexual morality and the quality of its offspring.

Human beings are mammals with a fairly long period of gestation and a very long period during which the child needs nurture. This long period of dependence of the child has been an important contributory factor to man's ascendancy over other animals. Ecological morality would seem to require respect and care for the pregnant woman and familial security for the child during the long period of 'bringing up'. If this conflicts with problems of selfhood in either or both of the parents these would seem to be of secondary importance and they should be resolved, not by separation but by other means such as tolerance and goodwill. Ecological morality requires of the individual, as the concomitant of participation, the acceptance of responsibility, and clearly the obligations attaching to many acts, including begetting a child, will continue over relatively long periods.

Ecological morality indicates a reappraisal of sexual practices and it seems probable that the quality of life will improve in communities which adopt a much more responsible attitude to the breeding and rearing of children.

Perhaps the greatest danger to the world ecosystem and to all its local component ecosystems is the population explosion. It will be a pity if police action has to be taken to prevent incontinent, overbreeding communities from overrunning their neighbours. It is to be hoped that personal acceptance of ecological responsibility leading to communal facilities and procedures will provide the essential compensation for man's achievement in removing the old painful checks upon population growth. There is an aspect of ecological morality which is as inexorable as the wrath of Jehovah, and the achievements of scientists in preserving life will be nullified and reversed by the simple and totally un-compassionate logic of nature unless we are able to act responsibly and effectively within a very short time.

Another matter in which ecological morality would seem to indicate a complete reassessment is violence. A great deal of what we regard as entertainment is ecologically obscene. Our atavistic obsession with violence as a solution to problems, or even as a way of life, is inimical to the ecological outlook in the modern context. Habituation to violent ways of thought may also appear to be contrary to social morality and the higher religions are opposed to it in theory if not in practice. Here again it is interesting to notice how quickly things are changing. Only a few years ago it would have been considered an outrage to show the birth of a child on television. Sexual obscenity has to a large extent been reassessed but so far only a few people see the common thriller or western as having an obscene content.

Ecological morality does not only pertain to the world outside ourselves. Each person is a unique organism which has to take its place in the environment. This requires not merely adjustment to the external environment but cultivation of the self in relation to external conditions. Thus in education there can be no standard formula because we are dealing with the relationship between two variables, the self and the ecosystem. The system can be altered by communal action in the interests of its inhabitants but the individual self has to make adjustments to the system. A realistic appraisal of what is possible within that system has to be made and this includes the possible variation in the system which may be brought about by the individual, within the context of ecological morality. The self should not be seen as an isolated and unrelated phenomenon, which it tends to be in the cases of people who feel that they are 'not wanted'. This can be seen as a breakdown in the ecological relationship of the individual to the environment, a relationship which it is the individual's responsibility to establish, though there is a reciprocal responsibility upon the community to cultivate the health of its participants. The first question the frustrated person should ask himself is what he has to offer, what he is giving. If there is a positive answer there is a beginning from which growth can take place. If the answer is negative he may need help. Here we touch upon psychology and psychotherapy the study of which, along with other life-sciences, seems to be essential for the development of ecological understanding of the human condition.

Finally there is the insubstantial environment created by ideas, art, transmitted skills, custom, education and the collective unconscious. Man is not a new phenomenon and he is not one generation deep. The effect of materialistic and rapacious selfishness has been to isolate people and to separate one generation from another. This is a morbid symptom of disease. We began by quoting Donne's saying that *'no man is an island, entire of itself: every man is a piece of the Continent, a part of the main'*. The continent is in time as well as space. We do not exist in one generation and it is of our nature that we are bridges between past and future. We inherit far more than we realize and are poor things apart from our inheritance, indeed we are meaningless.

The ecological outlook requires of us an awareness

of continuity as a positive value. By substituting the
garden for the machine as a model, we can abandon
the disgusting concept that each human being is a
standard product with an unrelated life-span. Instead
we can see that each plant in the garden is part of a
continuing living process and each seed-producing
flower has a genetic history which goes back millions
of years. But we must not be obsessed by the physical.
Continuity does not require of all of us that we should
plant our seed and beget physical heirs, indeed in our
present condition it is necessary that there should be
restraint of reproduction and probably, in some
societies at least, a degree of selectivity. The insubstantial environment of what Teilhard de Chardin
called the *noosphere*[50] (the sphere of mind) is enriched by all creative people: the good craftsman, the
mystic, the philosopher-physicist, the thoughtful
mother, the poet, the gardener. In a more leisured
society a new meaning can be given to life by increased
participation in and enjoyment of the collective inheritance. The art of contemplation, which has been
sadly neglected and almost lost in the rapacious
society, has much to offer to the individual man but
it requires self-discipline, cultivation and the power
to be attuned to the *noosphere*.

Chapter Seven

Responsibility to the Environment

We share Earth with other species. Some we cannot do without and for others we should have a sense of responsibility. The rapacious society, exploiting man and the rest of nature lacks a sense of responsibility and the blame does not belong to any one class of people but to all men. Economic values cannot be placed upon species. The reactionaries of the present time are the progress-at-all-costs money makers. In order to achieve a sensible ecological balance we need more knowledge and must encourage the best minds to study the life sciences.

We do not want to construct an *a priori* system but to recover the sense of exploration. To do this we must ensure freedom.

Man has become a major force in the ecology of Earth. He can be creative or destructive. Ecological morality rests upon a basic distinction between creativity and destruction, contribution and depredation. Man has trusteeship for nature. The exercise of this trusteeship depends upon his recovering the sense of respect which has been depraved in utilitarian industrial societies.

SUPPOSE MAN were able to eliminate all other forms of life on Earth he would be in a sorry plight. In fact human life would have become non-viable long before this point had been reached because, apart from the need for organic foods there are organisms which are necessary to our existence, such as the bacteria which deal with waste matter. Man could not survive as the sole form of life on Earth, so some kind of relationship with other life forms has to be accepted. We are compelled to reach some kind of compromise with other species quite apart from the aesthetic judgement that a world inhabited by man alone would be a much poorer place.

Until recently the problem of man using restraint of his own short term interests to preserve a balance with nature has mainly arisen in relation to hunting. If men want to hunt they must not over-kill or their sport will disappear with the extinction of the species they enjoy hunting. Ironically it is the hunters who have been the pioneers of conservation. The naturally predatory have been the first to realize that their predation must be limited. The pioneers of ecological conservation were, perhaps surprisingly, the medieval hunter-kings who established ferocious game laws. To the peasant of those days it looked like favouring deer at the expense of man and of course the peasants were right. The motive, to provide sport for the aristocracy, was corrupt but the principle of conservation was right. There is no need to reiterate here the grim story of the destruction of wild life by men armed with precision fire-arms but the process goes on and the menace now is not so much the unscrupulous hunter (though he still exists) as industry which, in the interests of economy, destroys by the billion creatures which never attracted anyone for sport or profit.

The rapacious society is bad enough in its exploitation of humanity for the sake of material gain but its industrial component is almost totally indifferent to the ecological damage it does in the pursuit of cost-effective gain. No industry is exempt from this stricture and even agriculture, which would seem to have a natural affinity for an ecological outlook, does in fact do immense ecological damage by the use of chemicals which seem to produce short-term advantages in crops and livestock but may pollute rivers and seas with disastrous results. They may also pollute the food which people eat but we still know very little about this because in the rapacious society, whatever the political formula, man is a subject for exploitation along with the other animals.[51]

The old grumble about the rich exploiting the poor is insignificant by comparison with the present reality of mankind as a whole exploiting mankind along with the rest of nature. The blame cannot be placed upon any small section of the community but belongs quite definitely to the main 'consumers', the proletariat. The more we proceed towards a 'fair' division of the spoils the greater blame accrues to the 'common people'. We are all to blame in this matter and the need is urgent to forget political animosities and recognize our collective participation in the impoverishment of the environment. Man is eating out his own heart by concentrating upon what we call economic gain without counting the real cost.

In economics value relates to the amount of one commodity that can be exchanged for another, whether the commodities be material or immaterial. In practice money becomes the medium of exchange but many values cannot be expressed in monetary terms. The aye-aye[52] is threatened as a species. It has taken millions of years to evolve this lovely creature but what financial value can possibly be placed upon its survival or extinction? The climate of the lower Tyne Valley in England is adversely affected by industrial plants at Blaydon which have toxic atmospheric effluents. Any doctor in the area will confirm that certain diseases are directly attributable to this pollution. It would be possible to add up the doctor's bills, hospital costs and loss of man hours due to these sicknesses in excess of the national average and set them against the cost of restraining and treating the effluent (this has not been done), but even so there would be the large element of human suffering, the generalized ill-health and lack of well-being, the destruction of plant and animal life among other considerations which could not be quantified in terms of money.

The assumption upon which we generally proceed is that 'progress must go on' and man is an adaptable animal capable of adapting to and putting up with conditions which are quite appalling so long as he does not actually drop dead on the spot when he enters the affected area. Industrialists, of course, will say it is a matter of common sense and that management share the same conditions as workers but in fact the environmental conditions are a function of, *maximum profit and the most that people will stand without actually refusing to work*. In the particular area under consideration (Tyneside) further development, and therefore regional prosperity is, in practice, affected by the reluctance of many people to work in the environment which exists. Such examples could

be given for almost any predominantly industrial area
and as we have noticed (p.26) industry creates low
environmental standards. This may, to some extent,
be inevitable but in a proper ecological assessment this
fact, if it is a fact, should be brought into account.
Certain ecological sacrifices may have to be made but
they should be recognized and set on the debit side.
The popular idea that 'development' means 'spoiling'
is not without foundation. If some areas have to be
spoiled this is a real *cost* and just as a person has to
achieve a balance in his own personal upkeep—his
food-intake, hygiene, sleep, indulgences such as alcohol
—so communities have to consider very carefully
whether development is acceptable. The reactionaries
in this context are the old progress-at-all-costs money
makers, not those who try to see the environmental
problem as a whole in accordance with an ecological
morality.

Somewhere between man degenerating into an
infestation, between man becoming the most
dangerous of vermin, and the self-balancing ecology
of regions uninhabited and unaffected by man, a
balance has to be struck. This cannot be done
spontaneously or by the obvious processes of democracy because in many areas ecological awareness has
become hopelessly depraved and in others it is still
primitively predatory. Immediately, the science of
man in relation to the rest of nature requires study
by the best minds. This study must cover many aspects,
not excluding the aesthetic aspect which concerns
man's *feeling* for and about his environment and his
emotional need for openness and non-human nature.
The crude value-judgements based upon profit are no

use to us any longer and we must reverse the materialistic thinking which has denied the relevance of value
judgements. We have to think in terms of relationships which are mutually affective. We need much
more subtle means of thinking and talking about
things and inevitably we have to evaluate compara-
tively. This implies higher standards of education in
new directions. It indicates an adventurous and hope-
ful future. This is a marked advantage which ecological thinking has over the materialism of the present
day.[53]

Throughout this book I have emphasized the
wrongness of constructing ideal systems *a priori* and
then working towards them. Instead we need to re-
capture the sense of adventure, of the unfolding of
what seems to be an infinite range of possibilities for
man which will probably lead, in a few hundred years,
to his becoming something which we would hardly
recognize as human at all, a being which would regard
us as being primitive indeed but probably worth preserving if colonies of us survive in out of the way
places! Having got over the sickness of nineteenth-
century ideas of progress, and tight nineteenth-century
models of thinking, we must become attuned to a
philosophy of growth[54] in which we ourselves as a
species exercise a specially significant role but cannot
exist in isolation.

It is not the purpose of this book to examine the
means but to indicate the moral basis for the growth
in quality of human existence. No one religion or
political system has a monopoly of truth and all con-
tain anachronisms and falsehoods. To free ourselves
from the present disillusion, frustration and impotent

anger which splits us into factions we cannot look to any political system as such. All political systems rest upon belief. They have to be credible in terms of values which people accept. But we have lost the sense of value. We have, as a species, temporarily[55] lost our way. The need is for a new morality and if this is accepted the political institutions will be created, as they have been in the past, to attempt to achieve what men want. The ecological answer to our political problem of improving our condition in the face of a threat to our existence is to propagate the ecological basis of morality and allow men to form the most active and effective communities to explore ways of achieving what we want. Such communities will necessarily be smaller than the large states of today and it would be against the nature of our morality to prescribe forms of government and administration. Various methods must be tried in different places and clearly some matters will require co-operation, federation or united action by all ecosystems. It is essential to outlaw war, for the reasons we have discussed, and if the creative spirit of man is to be most effectively liberated there must be complete freedom of political and religious belief, freedom from discrimination against colour, race, creed or opinion. It follows that there must be a distinction between opinion or belief and action based upon opinion or belief. To take an extreme case, a man may believe it is right to shoot all men with blond hair but if he acts upon this belief he has to be restrained in fairness to men with blond hair. Likewise the revolutionary who wants to weed other people's gardens is trespassing against ecological morality. It may seem that there is a danger here that society will stagnate but this is because we are so habituated to thinking about violent solutions in which men are divided against men. The violent revolutionary is an atavist, a reversionary. But once we rule out the possibility of war and violent attempts at the solution of differences of opinion or interest, creative minds are freed to act as a leaven. The extent to which this will be possible in any society will depend upon the quality of its people both by inheritance and culture. The danger in any such society is the demagogue, the 'con man' the advertiser for his own ends and the purveyor of falsehood through intent or incompetence, especially in the media of communication. The best disinfectant against such danger is wise and sceptical education. By sceptical I mean concerned with the truth behind appearances.[56]

The abandonment of war and the devolution of government to smaller communities in the context of an ecological morality would provide such a liberation of material and human creative resources that what now seems impossible would be achieved and new objectives which we cannot yet envisage would emerge. It is an advantage of ecological morality that it can suggest a brighter future instead of the gloomy prospects revealed by our present systems and beliefs.

For better or worse man has become a major force in the ecology of Earth. As a primitive species he was weak and vulnerable but he had upright posture, the use of his hands and a brain capable of development. As hunter and nomad he was part of the scenery and hard put to it to keep alive. When he settled he became, gradually, a marvellous cultivator. In the last two hundred years his knowledge and skills have increased to such an extent that he has powers which hitherto had been imagined as attributes of the gods; and recently he has gone far beyond the imaginative limits of the most fantastic myths of other days, though wise men in the past did discern some of the dangers of the path which western man has been following. Now he has the power to destroy the world he lives in, with all that inhabits it, but he also has the chance to play a creative role in the evolution of all living species including man himself as a species.

Human beings have always been aware of a difference between giving and taking away, between positive and negative and between good and evil. This last distinction is known to exist but is not so easy to define and has been confused by many entanglements with theology and social policy, but the stark dilemma of our own time, which has been created by the growth of man's power due to science and technology, opposes complete disaster and destruction as a very real possibility, to the alternative of an infinite development of living species under the guidance of man. Ecological morality has its basis in the distinction between destruction and creativity, between contribution and depredation.

In the long discussion about the validity of religion, which was stimulated by Charles Darwin's work on evolution and the origin of species, it has been a commonplace to ask why it is that if there is a good God he allows evil to exist in the world. I shall not enter this arena of discussion but, recognizing that it exists, one may see that the dilemma of God is now the dilemma of man. Why, if we believe in ourselves, do *we* permit evil things to happen? The answer lies partly in a failure to understand the logic and balance of nature, and partly in man, as a species with immense power, not accepting his responsibilities. Man has become proud (like Lucifer) and believes that he can 'go it alone' without any care for other creatures except as pets, because he likes to have them around, or because he likes to hunt. Except for microorganisms other species seem to have reached the end of an evolutionary road while man has the power to grow. He also has, in genetics, a key to the treasure house of evolved species. Just as there are minerals in the earth so there are living species whose genetic structure is the result of millions of years of creation. The thoughtless use of a chemical can destroy what can never be replaced and we have only begun to study this subject. Man has become the trustee for nature. As a trustee he can embezzle the funds and squander them, which by any commonsense standard is wicked, or he can invest wisely and cultivate the inheritance.

In the brash world of competitive industrialism and egalitarian materialism with its indiscriminate exploitation of the environment and of humanity, its ugly ghettos of housing for 'the workers' and its drab amusements, one of the principal casualties has been the sense of respect. We have great power and influence which we do not know how to use well. We are also extremely puny and personally ill-equipped. We cannot fly like the birds or swim like the fish but we have ingenious brains with which we can make up for our deficiencies and lumber about the world. Perhaps our greatest need is to recover the sense of awe, the sense of wonder, the gift for generously respecting that which is beautiful, true and excellent in all aspects of nature, not excluding ourselves and our fellow men.

Chapter Eight

Conclusion

IT MAY SEEM that we have wandered and reiterated, that we have considered but not concluded, that we have looked at a great many problems which vex the minds of thoughtful people but made no firm proposals. To set such a structure of contemplation and prejudice in favour of improving the human condition against the rational but limited and, it may now be agreed, out-dated dogmas of Marxism, against the doctrines of religions, against entrenched materialism, against the emergent nationalism of hitherto frustrated or backward peoples, against the generalized optimism of what survives of the liberal movement and, above all, against the idealization of human acquisitiveness which we call the capitalist system, may seem futile, and indeed it is. There comes a point in any investigation when a decision has to be made if its conclusions, final or provisional, are to be implemented in activity.

The decision finally takes place by pushing away all the arguments—both those that have been understood and others that might come up through further deliberation—and by cutting off all further pondering. The decision may be the result of deliberation, but it is at the same time complementary to deliberation: it excludes deliberation.[57]

Nothing is final, and throughout this book we have avoided conclusions, but in the present predicament

of mankind, which is desperate and dangerous, a provisional formulation of the new morality is necessary.
It is a basis for development, not a definitive statement if only because it envisages the further evolution
of man to a state of being in which a degree of understanding will be possible about which it would be
presumptuous and impertinent for any man now
living to say anything final.

With these reservations the practical conclusions of
our considerations are set out here, in the context of
our own time, as a manifesto, a necessary commitment
to belief embodied in action.

The living world is a unity. It is characterized by
the property of having life. Within it innumerable
species interact with their living and non-living
environment. Man is a component in this world ecosystem. He is a single species, directly dependent upon
many other species and, in his present partially civilized state upon irreplaceable materials which he is
consuming. As industrial man he has moved outside
the biological system of re-cycling and become a
predator upon the material substance of the earth
and upon all other species. He has reached a spawn-
ing stage and is rapidly becoming a horrifying infestation. Confronted with this terrible reality it becomes
a moral imperative, over-riding all other considerations, to re-establish the balance of the human species
in nature. Failure to do this will, (unless prevented by
a cataclysmic disaster to the whole of mankind such
as might rescue the rest of nature from him, but if
man has anything to do with its causation would more
likely destroy much of life on Earth), eliminate most

of the other advanced species and probably finish man
himself. Certainly everything worthy and beautiful
which man has created is at peril and anyone who
believes in the value of man, or anything man has
done, or is doing, must face up to the challenge.

Our new morality rests upon a natural imperative.
Man must accept the conditions of the world in which
he lives, the facts of life.

Man must establish and maintain a beneficial
relationship with the rest of nature. It cannot be
called beneficial unless it can be seen to extend per-
manently into the future. It must therefore be creative
not predatory. Conservation[58] is not enough.

All activities which pollute the earth or waste its
resources must come under scrutiny and be curtailed.
Population increase must be stopped.[59]

We must abandon as dangerous fantasy the delusion
that a technological miracle will solve our problems
while all the rest of nature seems to deserve a miracle
to destroy us. We are, as a species, getting deeper into
trouble every day that passes. The measure of our
descent is the growth of population and the growth of
the economy.

If there are moral imperatives we must consider the
means of obeying them.

We are one species. We must stop quarrelling. The
ridiculous dispute between socialists and capitalists
about how the spoils of exploitation should be admini-
stered and distributed must be abandoned. An entirely
new attitude is required on both sides. It is difficult
to see how capitalism based upon industry in a com-

petitive economy can survive. It will have to change beyond all recognition if certain real values which it enshrines are to be preserved into the future. Socialism, on the other hand, has created institutions which, although they are imperfect and directed at present towards exploitation, could be adapted to serve our ecological needs. To save ourselves and Earth, we need drastic economic changes and these can only be brought about within a controlled economy.

Both participants in the great irrelevance of our time, the confrontation of communism and capitalism, have established world-wide organizations for co-operation and consultation but everything is vitiated, at present, by the massed and menacing power of the two principal antagonists. The immediate need is for recognition that, in the face of a common danger, America and Russia must renounce war and disarm. This would immediately eliminate one of the greatest causes of waste.[60] Neither side can rule the world because the world cannot be ruled. Mankind has to learn to co-operate in the business of living here on Earth. To do this he must establish world wide organizations and agencies for specific purposes with consequent diminution of national sovereignty, but within this framework of functional organizations the present power structures and rights to veto must be demolished so that small communities may develop their potentialities in their own ways. The value of this is indicated, not only by the success of city states in the past and small nations in the present but also by the contrast between Russian satellites and the free communist societies in Yugoslavia and Cuba. It is essential that communities, whatever their form of government, should be of such size that their members can feel responsible for them and within them. The single voice must be able to make itself heard and anomy, the disease of the over-grown state, must be eliminated, partly because men are much happier when they feel responsible and able to participate, partly because, with such freedom, the intellectual, social, artistic and skilful potentialities of people have a chance to flower and enrich the world. We are back to our garden analogy. We need to create a system of human co-operation wherein each community can cultivate a different kind of garden and make it productive.

In the long term, with inevitably diminishing supplies of minerals the nightmare of industrial automation begins to fade. Inexorably the industrial revolution is destroying itself. It is our concern to make sure that it does not destroy everything else and suddenly it has become clear, in the nineteen seventies, that the old 'progressives' are now the reactionaries and the new objective is to restore quality to life.

It is fair to ask, since we are talking about morality, what this means in terms of human behaviour. The answer is quite simple, it means feeling responsible towards the community in which one lives and trying to contribute more than one takes out. It means respect for life and confidence in the future. The reward of faith in the future is a sense that one's contribution is not in vain.

If we do not accept a new morality we can have no confidence in the future and we shall be condemned to alienation and misery. It is a psycho-physical necessity for us to believe, and as things are now we cannot believe in the future of man unless we take action.

NOTES

Chapter 1. *Introduction.*

1. Russell, B.: *History of Western Philosophy*, p. 10. 1946.
2. Donne, J.: *Devotions*, 1624.
3. Shakespeare, *Macbeth*.
4. This Christian-Socialist attitude is, of course, in marked contrast to such injunctions as *Let him deny himself, and take up his cross and follow me.* (Matt. 16:24).
5. Blake, William: from *Milton*, 1804.
6. See Allsopp, Bruce: *Civilization, the Next Stage*, 1969, p. 51 sqq.
7. American Declaration of Independence 1776.

Chapter 2. *The Functional Nature of Morality in Relation to Modern Conditions.*

8. Smith, V. R.: *Classical Dictionary.*
9. Kipling, Rudyard: *Recessional.*
10. Dyer, John: *Here's a health to the King*, early eighteenth century.
11. Browning, R.: *Childe Roland to the Dark Tower Came.*
12. It is often argued that *because* we may undergo some great disaster such as a plague we must keep up the birthrate, but now the birthrate is itself the cause of probable disaster, not the insurance against it. It would only be *after* a disaster that current Roman Catholic dogma on this matter could become acceptable; at present it is likely to contribute to disaster. This is an interesting example of how morality must be related to conditions as they are.
13. This functional view of morality is, of course, open to some objections and is certainly incomplete (see, for example, Durkheim's work) but in this book we are concerned with a functional morality for modern society and it is upon this aspect of ethics that we have to concentrate.

14. Environment, as will be noted later, is both internal and external. Our condition of anomy is not only due to disharmony with the external world but also derives from a sense of place-lessness within ourselves.

15. Reported by Pearce Wright in *The Times*, 7th September 1971.

Chapter 3. *Conditions for an Ecological Morality.*

16. Ullswater, English Lake District.

17. Arnold, Matthew: *In Harmony with Nature*, 1849.

18. Santayana, George, 1863-1952. In Pritchard, F. H. (Ed.) *Essays of Today*, London 1923.

Chapter 4. *The Garden Analogue.*

19. Stuart, G. M. in *Chambers Encyclopedia*.

20. Gaea was the personification of Earth, the earth goddess and her gift of fruit was to Hera, the consort of Zeus, the chief of the gods.

21. Howard, E.: *Tomorrow*, 1898.

22. Joll, J.: *The Anarchists*, 1964.

23. Godwin, W.: *Enquiry Concerning Political Justice*, 1793. This was a pioneer work of optimistic political anarchism.

24. It is becoming clear that industry has immense problems ahead, particularly in relation to raw materials. Our present economic system is creaking and if, as seems likely, we eventu-ally go on to a commodity standard as the basis of currency, as Nicholas Kaldor has proposed, the relationship of manufactur-ing to the production of raw materials will change drastically in favour of primary producing countries. Furthermore, exploita-tion is creating shortages and prices are rising steeply. A more economical and waste-saving attitude to industry may be en-forced by rising material costs but will be too slow to restore the ecological balance before it is too late.

Chapter 5. *Man and the Environment.*

25. The consequences and conditions are well established in Eyre, S. R.: *Population, Production and Pessimism*, British Association for the Advancement of Science, 1971.

26. See pp. 4, 37, 105 and note 40.

27. Published 1933. The idea has, of course, become a commonplace of popular science fiction.

28. The philosophy of Hegel is interesting in this respect, especially his idea of God fulfilling himself through man. Marx derived a great deal of his influence upon the subsequent course

of history from being tuned-in to holistic philosophies and being able to exclude everything outside his own system as hostile, irrelevant or really non-existent.

29. Heisenberg, W.: *Physics and Philosophy—The Revolution in Modern Science*, London, 1959, p. 172.

30. Political theory usually underestimates man and over-simplifies him.

31. Engels was naïve in saying 'the former division of labour must disappear . . . there will no longer be any professional porters or architects and . . . the man that for half an hour gives instructions as an architect will also push a barrow for a period'. (Engels, F.: *Selected Works I*, p. 102). This is a good example of the point made in note 30.

32. Buckminster Fuller is the principal protagonist.

33. As Eyre has shown (*op. cit.* in note 25) the greatest excess is in the non-industrial countries and is already at the threshold of famine. There is no possibility of sustaining the present increase of population by agriculture or industry.

34. This idea is proposed in my *Civilization, the Next Stage. op. cit.* Note 6.

35. Both communist and non-communist. The gloom which has eclipsed Czechoslovakia since its incorporation in Russia is significant.

36. Good may come from surprising sources. The increasing internationalization of industry is creating world-wide agencies and uni-functional administrative systems which may be useful in an ecological world order.

37. 'A normal living organism is an orderly integrated succession of enzyme reactions.' Hewitt, J. A. in *Chambers Encyclopedia*.

38. Here it is interesting to take a Marxist view of 'progressiveness': 'The society which is judged to be progressive, and so worthy of support, is that which is capable of further expansion in its initial direction without an alteration of its entire basis. A society is reactionary when it is inevitably moving into an impasse, unable to avoid internal chaos and ultimate collapse in spite of the most desperate efforts to survive, efforts which create irrational faith in its own ultimate stability the anodyne with which all dying institutions necessarily delude themselves.' Berlin, Isiah. *Karl Marx—His Life and Environment*, p. 11.

If this is a fair statement of the Marxist view the ecological crisis suggests a rethinking of communism if it is to avoid 'moving into an impasse'. The same is true of course, for capitalist society. We need a new society with a new moral basis.

39. But see *Conclusion*, p. 104.

40. We must not make the mistake, which was natural to nineteenth-century thinkers with their mechanistic models and cramped horizons, of predetermining the course of history and the potentialities of man. These people were capable of a cosmic arrogance which their uncritical followers continue to practice but it is outrageous to the modern mind which has new tools to think with. Among the most important of these are the idea of relativity, the concept of a continuum, complementarity, ecology and genetics.

Unfortunately German philosophy, from Kant to Hegel and M..rx, was dominated by the limited equipment of brilliant academic minds which had, by modern standards, remarkably little knowledge of the world. They constructed mental empires which, as such, command respect, but, apart from their limited horizons in the context in which they lived, practically everything they 'knew' about the environment, in a scientific sense, was inadequate or has since been proved wrong. (e.g. Marx's ideas were crystalized by 1850, nine years before the publication of Darwin's *Origin of Species*). They lived in a simple world where apples fell on physicists and proved the law of gravity. It is no longer like that. We have learned that the act of looking at something may alter it. Relativity was beyond Marx's horizon and the concept of anti-matter, crudely described as a symmetrical relationship between what is and what is not would have seemed mystical rather than a serious part of physics. The work of Pasteur and Lister on germs and antiseptics was still to come.

We have been dominated and imprisoned for far too long by thinkers whose intellectual furniture is now totally out of date and the world of nature, as revealed so far by modern science, is no longer one of simply stated principles but, at the level of our experience, an infinitely complicated system of inter-relationships of material things which, when analysed, seem to be assembled out of components made of 'insubstantial' energy. The distinction between the abstract and the concrete, or 'real', has become much less clear than it was in the nineteenth century.

41. Some kind of international police force has to be envisaged. Its successful operation must depend upon: (a) the formulation of a body of international law, and (b) the absence of any power strong enough to over-ride international law. The present weakness of the United Nations is due to the major powers being unwilling to accept the judgements of an international court. Therefore the blame for international anarchy

rests not upon the small nations but upon those powers which claim a right of veto. These are the reactionary powers so far as international law is concerned. They can only claim the 'right' of veto because they are too powerful—because, in ordinary parlance, they are bullies.

Chapter 6. *Ecological Morality and the Individual.*

42. Demonstration has become a characteristic means of making opinion known in societies where effective communication between people and government has broken down. Most demonstrations are honest but, like anything else, the demonstration technique can be prostituted and used corruptly.

43. cf. page 1.

44. In fact it would not work because the daisies in isolation would destroy the suitability of the environment for daisies by over-exploiting and polluting it.

45. Clausewitz, Karl von, 1780-1831: *Vom Kriege (On War)*, published posthumously, 1832.

46. This 'good-doing' even extends to time bombs in schools, indiscriminate ambushes and ritual murder.

47. An extreme example of the loss of a sense of proportion is The British Redcliffe Maud Report, which proposes to concentrate effective power in conurbations and sever them from the country.

48. See note 40.

49. Penguin Dictionary of Biology (also on p. 56).

50. de Chardin, Teilhard, *The Phenomenon of Man.* 1959.

Chapter 7. *Responsibility to the Environment.*

51. It must be emphasized that it is not capitalism but industrial society that is to blame. In the 'advanced' countries we all share in the blame. Class has nothing to do with it.

52. Aye-aye *(Daubentonia Madagascariensis)*, a squirrel-like animal which is nearly extinct. It used to be sacred, but now it is being killed for alleged damage to coconut plantations. The main threat is commercial destruction of its habitat. See Fisher, J., Simon N., Vincent, J.: *The Red Book: Wildlife in Danger*, London, 1969, p. 38.

53. Generally ecology is associated with pessimism (as in Eyre *op. cit.* note 25) but the pessimistic presentation corresponds to a paradisal possibility if we heed the warnings in time.

54. Not, of course, economic growth as at present understood but something much more like 'growth in grace'.

55. The word *temporarily* is optimistic.

56. This implies a raising of intellectual standards in education.

Chapter 8. *Conclusion.*

57. Heisenberg, W.: *Physics and Philosophy*, p. 175.

58. Conservation as at present understood is only a gradual retreat.

59. This is an over-riding imperative. The *means* must be worked out and applied within every expanding community. Birth control, sterilization, euthanasia, suicide, abortion, a tax on children, legal restriction of the right to breed, legal restraints upon marriage and, above all, a new climate of opinion, new customs, but the methods must follow conviction and be appropriate to the societies in which they are adopted. Leadership should be expected from the intellectually developed countries.

60. And some of the major sources of pollution.

Index

sympathy, 44

Technology, 3, 14, 64, 75, 99
thalidomide, 29
third level morality, 72, 73
Times, The, 26, 108
toleration, 5
trade union, 8, 75
tradition, 67
trusteeship, 91
Tyne, 94

Ullswater, 32, 108
United Nations, 69, 110

Varieties, 49
variety, of talent, etc., 62
value judgement, 24, 40, 50,
51, 52, 54, (66), 95, 96
values, vii, 5, 9, 14, 17, 22, 24,
25, 26, 29, 52, 55, 62

vandals, 44
Versailles, 22, 43
Vietnam, 59, 83
violence, 36, 63, 73, 88, 98
Virgil, 20
Voltaire, 45, (66)

Wales, 26, 67,
war, 2, 11, 14, 16, 28, 35, 36,
37, 40, 47, 59, 63, 64, 83, 98,
105
waste, 64, 74
wealth, 8, 22, 28
Wells, H. G., 58
work, workers, 7, 9, 22, 28, 75,
100
world-state, 65, 84

Yugoslavia, 105